COMMUNITY DEVELOPMENT
AN OUTREACH APPROACH

COMMUNITY DEVELOPMENT
AN OUTREACH APPROACH

M.P. Boraian

ANMOL PUBLICATIONS PVT. LTD.
NEW DELHI - 110 002 (INDIA)

ANMOL PUBLICATIONS PVT. LTD.
H.O.: 4374/4B, Ansari Road, Daryaganj,
New Delhi-110 002 (India)
Ph.: 23278000, 23261597
B.O.: No. 1015, Ist Main Road, BSK IIIrd Stage
IIIrd Phase, IIIrd Block,
Bangalore - 560 085 (India)
Visit us at: www.anmolpublications.com

Community Development: An Outreach Approach

ISBN 978-81-261-3661-2

PRINTED IN INDIA

Printed at Mehra Offset Press, Delhi.

CONTENTS

PREFACE

India continues to be a global economic power, ranking as the 12th largest economy in the world. India is home for a couple of wealthiest persons in the world, and ranks fourth in the world's list of dollar billionaires. Nevertheless, 25 per cent of India's 1.1 billion people have yet to notice positive improvements from economic development in their own lives. An estimated 300 million persons currently live below poverty line, with 200 millions surviving on less than US $ 2 per day.

India occupies 126th position in respect of Human Development Index (HDI) with a HDI value of 0.611among the 177 countries ranked by the UNDP (2006). Norway stands first (0.965) while Niger occupies the last place (0.311). In respect of Gender related Development Index (GDI), India was placed in the 98th position among the countries with a GDI value of 0.586 (as against 0.960, the highest for Norway and 0.311, the lowest for Burkina Faso.) Recent survey findings show that 46 per cent of Indian children suffer from malnutrition.

These facts suggest that India's recent economic gains have succeeded in enriching the social elite and the middle classes, and they have failed to benefit atleast one-third of the country's population. Government of India have allotted over Rs. 30,000 crore under XI Five Year Plan for rural development. A galaxy of path breaking poverty alleviation and employment generation programmes such as National Rural Employment Guarantee Scheme, SGSY, etc. have been under implementation across the country.

Yet, the magnitude of the problem and the quantum of resources seldom match, resulting in the need for additional institutions and abundant resources for cracking rural backwardness and crushing rural poverty. Supplementing, supporting and even surpassing the government's efforts in rural development are Non-Government Organisations, Corporates, Public Sector undertakings, banks, hospitals, schools, colleges and universities.

Four major sectors - *viz.*, Government, NGOs, Private sector and the academic institutions have been undertaking various measures to reach out to the rural communities in order to address their problems and redress their grievances. In pursuit of their rural outreach mission, they use a plethora of approaches, strategies, programmes, methodologies, management systems and resource packages. What are their philosophies, activities and methods of reaching out to people? How do they differ from the others and outsmart each other? What are their successes and failures and the reasons thereof?

Precisely to find answers to these pivotal questions, a three day National Seminar was held at Gandhigram Rural University (GRU) on "Community Outreach Methodologies – The Dimensions and Dilemmas," on the eve of GRU's Golden Jubilee celebrations during August 2006. Participating institutions represented Government, Nationalised banks, Non-Government Organisations, Colleges, Universities, Consultancy Organisations and Donor agencies. Resource persons comprised activists, academicians, government officials, heads of donor agencies from overseas, development consultants, scientists, and research scholars.

A total of 26 resource persons are arranged under specific headings *viz.*, Concept and Dimensions, outreach by colleges and universities, children-centered outreach, outreach among women and youth, outreach among farmers, experiments in rural outreach and outreach in other states. This is a maiden attempt of Department of Extension Education, Gandhigram Rural University to bring out a publication of this much practiced but less preached and professed theme Community Outreach. Comments and suggestions are welcome from the readers.

Gandhigram M.P. BORAIAN

वी. एस. सम्पत
महानिदेशक
V.S. SAMPATH
DIRECTOR GENERAL

राष्ट्रीय ग्रामीण विकास संस्थान
ग्रामीण विकास मंत्रालय, भारत सरकार का संगठन
राजेन्द्रनगर, हैदराबाद - 500 030
NATIONAL INSTITUTE OF RURAL DEVELOPMENT
An Organisation of the Ministry of Rural Development Government of India
Rajendranagar, Hyderabad - 500 030

FOREWORD

In recent years, major changes have occurred in the methods and concept of self-reliance and sustainability in rural development. One of the most crucial interventions in the development of the poor and the marginalized is the outreach methodologies. The term 'outreach' as it is used today, covers a fairly wide range of strategies and approaches, some quite different from each other, but all aimed at providing services to those who otherwise remain unreached. Outreach is an effort by an organization or group to connect its ideas or practices to the efforts of other organizations, groups, specific audiences or the general public. Unlike marketing, outreach does not inherently revolve round a product or strategies to increase market share. Typically non-profits, civic groups, and churches engage in outreach.

Outreach often takes on an educational component (i.e., the dissemination of ideas), but it is increasingly common for organizations to conceive of their outreach strategy as a two-way street in which outreach is framed as engagement rather than solely dissemination or education. Outreach strategies are linked to the organization's mission, and define targets, goals, and milestones.

Outreach programmes, however, are not a panacea. So far, only a few have been able to sustain themselves beyond five years. Many, initially hailed as successful, have turned out to be long-term failures and most 'model' programmes have not been easy to replicate in other settings or work environments; the reasons for this are still poorly understood. As more and better use is made of these bridging strategies, we should try to learn, through operational research, how to have an even greater impact.

How does one define a good outreach programme? How does one initiate one where none exists, but its need is fully justified? We are still awaiting conclusive evidence on what makes a good outreach programme, its long-term success and benefits, and its replicability. However, lessons learned and experience gleaned over the years would suggest the essential elements for any outreach programme.

With a view to finding answers to these pivotal questions, a three-day national seminar was organized at Gandhigram rural University on 'Community Outreach Methodologies - The Dimensions and Dilemmas' in August 2006. Dr. M.P. Boraian has edited this book by compiling the seminar papers. It is expected that this book on 'community outreach methodologies' will serve as a reference tool for students, policy makers, administrators, experts and civil society institutions and others in reaching out to rural communities in order to address their problems and redress their grievances.

V.S. Sampath

(V. S. Sampath)
Director General
National Institute of Rural Development (NIRD), Hyderabad.

ACKNOWLEDGEMENT

I am thankful to the University Grants Commission, Ministry of Human Resource Development, Government of India for sponsoring the three day National Seminar on "Community Outreach Methodologies – The Dimensions and Dilemmas" on the eve of Gandhigram Rural University's Golden Jubilee celebrations during August 2006.

I am grateful to the former Vice-Chancellors of Gandhigram Rural University viz., Dr. N. Markandan, Dr. Ms. G. Pankajam and Dr. T. Karunakaran, the Registrar Dr. M. Sundaravadivelu and Dr. N. Narayanasamy, Professor and Head, Dept. of Extension Education and Dean, Faculty of Rural Development who were instrumental in organising this seminar at various stages.

I wish to thank COMIC RELIEF, a funding agency in U.K, which has co-sponsored the seminar through its Indian partner ICT-SEEDS Trust, headed by Mr. Rajkumar. My thanks are due to Toshihiro Yoneyama, Director, LIFE (Living with Friends on the Earth, a funding agency from Japan, and Mr. S. Alexander, Regional Advisor, Asia Pacific Team, Protestant Churches, Netherlands

I record my sincere thanks to the team of distinguished resource persons and participants – Dr. R. Mohanraj (Bangalore), Ms. R. Bhanumathi (Chennai), Development Consultants, Prof. R. Subramanian, Prof. P.K. Kothandapani, and Dr. A. Suriakanthi, former Deans, Faculty of Rural Development and Heads of Departments Dr. N. Kamalamma (Home Science), Dr. N. Thillainayagam (RIM), Dr. B.R. Dwaraki (Sociology), Dr. S. Ramachandran (Economics), and Dr. M.A. Sudhir (Applied Research) who chaired the sessions and offered valuable insights.

Dr. S. Lakshmi, Reader, Faculty of English and Foreign Languages helped in going through the entire draft and I am immensely thankful to her for her painstaking effort. I thank Dr. N. Narayanasamy, once again for going through this work and offering his valuable comments.

Technical support extended by a band of 14 young Faculties and energetic Research Scholars as Rapporteurs, able administrative support provided by Mr. C. Asokumar, Dr. E. Perumal and efficient secretarial support offered by Ms. B.Vani, Sri. R. Saravanan and Sri. P. Sellachamy are invaluable and I owe my deep sense of gratitude to each one of them.

M.P.BORAIAN

LIST OF CONTRIBUTORS

ALEXANDAR, S	: Regional Advisor, Asia Pacific Team, United Protestant Churches (Netherlands), Madurai, TN.
ANTONI, M.P	: Project Manager, CASP Project, Rajagiri College of Social Sciences, Rajagiri, Kochin, Kerala.
ARUNACHALAM, R	: Assistant Professor, Dept. of Agriculture Extension & Rural Sociology, Agriculture College and Research Institute (ACRI), Tamil Nadu Agriculture University (TNAU), Madurai, TN.
BALASUBRAMANIYAN, V	: Director, Avinashilingam Jan Shikshan Sansthan, Coimbatore, T.N.
BHANUMATHI, R	: Development Consultant for Donor Agencies, Chennai, T.N.
BINOY JOSEPH	: Lecturer, Dept. of Social Work, Rajagiri Colleges of Social Sciences, Rajagiri, Kochin, Kerala.
BORAIAN, M.P	: Professor, Dept. of Extension Education, Gandhigram Rural University (GRU), Gandhigram, T.N.
EASWARAN, A	: Reader, Dept. of Extension Education, GRU, Gandhigram, T.N.
GANESAN, R	: Professor (Agrl. Extn.), Dept. of Agricultural Extension & Rural Sociology, TNAU, Coimbatore. T.N.
KAMALAMMA, N	: Former Professor and Head, Dept. of Home Science, GRU, Gandhigram, T.N.
KAVITHA @ MAITHILY, S	: Lecturer, Dept. of Home Science, GRU, Gandhigram, T.N.

KRISHNASAMY, C	: Project Co-ordinator, SHGs Micro Enterprises Project, Gandhigram Trust, Gandhigram, T.N.
MAHENDRAKUMAR, K	: Assistant Professor, Dept. of Agricultural Extension and Rural Sociology, AC & RI, Madurai, T.N.
MANI, N.D	: Professor & Head, Dept. of Rural Development, GRU, Gandhigram, T.N.
MANIKANDAN, K	: Lecturer in Economics, Dept. of Economics, GRU, Gandhigram, T.N.
MANIVANNAN, A	: Assistant professor, Dept. of Veterinary & Animal Husbandry Extension, Veterinary College & Research Institute, VCRI, Namakkal, T.N.
MATHIALAGAN, P	: Associate Professor and Head, Dept. of Veterinary and Animal Husbandry Extension VCRI, Namakkal, T.N.
MOHAN RAJ, R	: Development Consultant, Bangalore.
NARAYANASAMY. N	: Professor & Head, Dept. of Extension Education and Dean, Faculty of Rural Development, GRU, Gandhigram, T.N.
NIRMALA, L.	: Teaching Assistant, Agriculture College and Research Institute, TNAU, Madurai, T.N.
PADMINI BALAGOPAL	: Site Coordinator, TAMRF-GRI Project, GRU, Gandhigram, T.N.
PALANITHURAI, G	: Professor and Head, Dept. of Political Science, GRU, Gandhigram, T.N.
RAJKUMAR, T	: Project Director, ICT-India Project, Dindigul, T.N.
RAMAKRISHNAN, K	: Teaching Assistant, (Agri. Extn.) AC & RI, Killikulam, Valanad, T.N.
RANJITA MISRA	: Principal Investigator, TAMRF-GRI Project, Texas A & M University, U.S.A.
SAKUNTHALAI, A	: Assistant Professor, Agricultural Extension, Coastal Saline Research Centre, TNAU, Ramanathapuram, T.N.

SEKAR, V	: Professor and Head, Dept. of Agricultural Extension and Rural Sociology, TNAU, Madurai, T.N.
SREEKANTAN THAMPI, P.S	: Deputy Director, Spices Board of India, Eranakulam, Kerala (President of Jana Jagritha Samithi).
SURIAKANTHI, A	: Director, Dept. of Adult Continuing Education and Extension, GRU, Gandhigram, T.N.
THANGAMANI SWAMINATHAN	: Professor and Head, Dept. of Home Science Extension Education, Avinashilingam University for Women, Coimbatore, T.N.
USHA RANI, S	: Development Officer, Rubber Board, Kottayam, Kerala.

ABBREVIATIONS AND ACRONYMS USED

AAPI	:	American Association of Physicians of Indian Origin
AC & RI	:	Agriculture College and Research Institute
ADD	:	Action on Disability and Development
AICRP	:	All India Coordinated Research Project
APCD	:	Asia Pacific Centre on Disability
AWTC	:	Anganwadi Training Centre
BDO	:	Block Development Officer
BMI	:	Body Mass Index
CACL	:	Campaign Against Child Labour
CAPART	:	Council for People's Action and Rural Technology
CASP	:	Community Aid and Sponsorship Programme
CBOs	:	Community based Organisations
CRC	:	Convention on the Rights of the Child
CRRC	:	Child Rights Resource Centre
CSIs	:	Civil Society Institutions
CSR	:	Corporate Social Responsibility
CSSR	:	Centre for Soil Salinity Research

DANIDA	:	Danish International Development Agency
DIC	:	District Industries Centre
DRDA	:	District Rural Development Agency
DTP	:	Desktop Publishing
EDP	:	Entrepreneurship Development Programme
ESCAP	:	Economic and Social Commission for Asia and the Pacific
GDI	:	Gender related Development Index
GRU	:	Gandhigram Rural University
HDI	:	Human Development Index
HUDCO	:	Housing and Urban Development Corporation
ICAR	:	Indian Council for Agriculture Research
ICMR	:	Indian Council for Medical Research
ICSSR	:	Indian Council for Social Science Research
ICSW	:	Indian Council of Social Welfare
ICT	:	International Childcare Trust
IDARA	:	Information Development and Resource Agency
IDRC	:	International Development Research Centre
IFG	:	Impaired Fasting Glucose

IPE	:	Institute of People's Education
IPR	:	Intellectual Property Rights
JSS	:	Jan Shikshan Sansthan
KVIC	:	Kadhi and Village Industries Commission
KVK	:	Krishi Vigyan Kendra
LIFE	:	Living with Friends on the Earth
MLTC	:	Micro Level Training Centre
MSSRF	:	M.S.Swaminathan Research Foundation
NAAC	:	National Assessment and Accreditation Committee
NCRI	:	National Council for Rural Institutes
NERD	:	Non-conventional Energy for Rural Development
NGDO	:	Non-Government Development Organisation
NGO	:	Non-Government Organisation
NPE	:	National Policy on Education
NSS	:	National Service Scheme
NTPC	:	National Thermal Power Corporation
ORT	:	Oral Rehydration Theraphy
PIA	:	Principal Implementing Agency
PRA	:	Participatory Rural Appraisal
SGSY	:	Sambooran Gram Swaraj Yojana
SHG	:	Self Help Group

SIDA	:	Swedish International Development Agency
TANWA	:	Tamil Nadu Women in Agriculture Programme
TNCDW	:	Tamil Nadu Corporation of Development of Women
TOC	:	Training and Orientation Centre
UAS	:	University of Agricultural Sciences
UGC	:	University Grants Commission
UNDP	:	United Nations Development Programme
UNESCO	:	United Nations Economic, Social & Cultural Organisation
UNFPA	:	United Nations Population Fund
UNICEF	:	United Nations Children Fund
VHAI	:	Voluntary Health Association of India
WDT	:	Watershed Development Team
WEI	:	Women Empowerment Index
WHO	:	World Health Organisation
WTO	:	World Trade Organisation

COMIC RELIEF

Comic Relief was set up in 1985 by comedians who wanted to do something to help others. Using comedy and laughter, it raised money to change lives – while making sure that everyone had great fun at the same time. Comic Relief's vision is a just world, free from poverty. The mission is to drive positive change through the power of entertainment. Over the years, more than two thousand celebrities have given their time and talent to Comic Relief Comic Relief.

International Childcare Trust, U.K.

International Childcare Trust (ICT) was founded in 1982 by David Lamont, on the concepts of empowerment and child-centered, active participation. ICT works to protect children's rights within a community development context. The children, their families and their communities are always involved in the decisions that shape ICT's programmes.

ICT exists for the purposes of eradicating poverty and protecting the basic rights of children and young persons as set out in the United Nations Convention on the Rights of the Child, particularly by preventing and relieving sickness and advancing the education of children and young persons anywhere in the world who are in condition of need, hardship or distress. ICT achieves these objectives by designing, implementing and managing projects in conjunction with local people, according to their needs and within the culture of the country of operation. Projects are managed and staffed by local people.

ICT provides practical help and aid to children in developing countries either through direct action with the child or through projects that assist the families of children. Projects cover primary health care, income generation schemes, rehabilitation centres for displaced children and many other aspects of support. Most of the activities are funded by grants from government organisations, UK and European trusts and donations from businesses and individuals.

It has two major fundraising campaigns: Red Nose Day and Sport Relief. Red Nose Day is a UK-wide fundraising event organised by Comic Relief every two years which culminates in a night of extraordinary comedy and moving documentary films. It's the biggest TV fundraising event in the UK calendar. On Red Nose Day everyone in England, Scotland, Wales and Northern Ireland is encouraged to cast inhibitions aside, put on a Red Nose, and do something a bit silly to raise money – celebrities included.

Sport Relief harnesses the power of sport to change lives for the better, where hundreds of thousands of people across the country take to the streets to raise cash. The money raised is spent by Comic Relief to help vulnerable people living incredibly tough lives both at home in the UK and in the world's poorest countries. Both these events that unite the entire nation in trying to make a difference to the lives of thousands of individuals facing terrible injustice or living in abject poverty.

Comic Relief is obviously a charity – but it's also a business too. On the business side of things, Comic Relief works with key corporate partners to produce products and promotions that are profitable.

Chapter 1

The Journey of Outreach- A Synthesis

M.P. Boraian

In the galaxy of jargons related to rural development, we deal with concepts like change agents, target communities, stakeholders, interventions, approaches, strategies, methods, input, output, outcome, impact, sustainability and so on. 'Outreach' has joined this array of concepts, not recently though. It refers to a process by which change agents reach out to the target communities by designing certain mechanisms and methodologies to facilitate their outreach process. Outreach may be referred to as a bridge that connects the change agents and clientele population, a conduit to channelise the ideas and inputs to the target community, and a means of sharing the agencies of and responses of the beneficiaries.

In the process, both the intervening institutions and intervened community learn, either successes or failures or a blend of both. With these lessons, both of them try to outsmart each other-by minimising the failures and maximising the successes by the agency, and reducing the losses and increasing gains by the community. In the process, certain outreach agencies keep changing their less successful methodologies, while the shrewd communities keep changing the less gainful agencies. Ultimately, what remains in balance from both, constitute the outreach design, process and outcome.

Concept and Dimensions

The concept of outreach and its various dimensions are clearly defined by Boraian. Community outreach is defined as a mission, a mandate, a programme, or a process, deliberately designed by change agents in order to solve the basic problems of a group or community, through a multitude of approaches, strategies and methods in the socio-cultural setting of the target population. Outreach activities, though undertaken by a plethora of agencies, outreach by university / college is emphasised in this work more elaborately. In an academic setting, outreach takes several forms–teaching outreach, research outreach, consultancy outreach, and service outreach. Treating outreach as similar to Extension and Engagement, gives a model outreach log is given for use by outreach workers.

Outreach has to be linked to the concept of self reliance, sustainability in development and replicability, says Mohanraj. Change agents of various kind such as the corporates, and academic institutions have a concern for the people below poverty line and express their concern through action, by predominantly investing their own resources and supplement from other sources through networking. On the other hand, NGOs work in collaboration with Government and Resource organisations, whose mission is development work, by implementing development projects for the stakeholders. Their methodology involves a planned input – output and impact (IOI) sequences. He outlines three types of relationship between the promoter (i.e. target outreach agency) and the stakeholder (i.e. community) *viz.*, promoter-driven, stakeholder-driven and partnership-based.

People are vulnerable not only to problems, issues and exploitations but also to different types of development propositions brought out by change agents for participation by the people, says Alexander. Most of the development methodologies such as BM seeds, shrimp farming, and SHG formations over-emphasise economic empowerment but ignore other factors such as environmental and ecological protection. Many a development approaches have resulted in short term gains but contributed to negative impact in the long run. He calls for a wholistic view of development encompassing all dimensions including social, political, environmental, and Human rights, so that any outreach effort will be fruitful.

Outreach takes place when a change agent works 'for', or 'thro' or 'with' or 'among' the community say Narayanasamy and Boraian. They observe that proximity with the community in the outreach process decides the extent of involvement of the community – the least in 'for' model to less in 'thro' model, and 'more' in 'with' model to 'most' in the 'among' model. Arguing that working 'with and among' is better than working 'through and for' the community, the authors claim that the 'least' participative models are 'outreach agency dominant' whereas the 'most' participative models are 'community – dominant'.

It documents the experience of three major outreach programmes of Gandhigram Rural University viz., university at the village doorsteps (rural stay by students and teachers), quadrangular approach in grassrooot planning (by community, university, government and the bank) and Participatory Rural Appraisal (PRA), propounded by Robert Chambers and implemented by the Gandhigram University, all these three programmes involve both the teachers and students to work 'with and among' the people rather than merely work 'for and through' people.

Outreach, in view of Narayanasamy is development oriented and strongly promotes the concept of equity and sustainability in order to create a self-reliant community. The more choice and flexibility that development facilitators have in their development strategies, the greater their ability to facilitate the process of development. The author lists out some of these strategies which include: Participatory research, Methodological pluralism, Think and link micro to macro, build social capital, build, operate and turn out Civil Society Institutions (CSIs), establish linkages between institutions and putting the first last.

Outreach by Universities

Even after 60 years of democratic governance, and implementation of rural development schemes for the poor, people still live in sub-human conditions; on the contrary, the number of educational institutions are on the rise, laments Palanithurai. All the higher educational institutions have several extendable aspects such as information, knowledge, skills, technology, service and so on. Many institutions do not have the mechanism to convert the available extendables suitable to the requirements of the community, and hence he has suggested a 'framework of outreach' integrated with their curriculum, for implementation by educational institutions.

The resources for education are the inputs from the community says, Thangamani Swaminathan. She has documented the various outreach methodologies followed by Sri Avinashilingam Deemed University, (TN) through the hierarchy of educational institutions *viz.*, pre-school, primary school, higher secondary school, college and the university. Various approaches viz., individual, group and mass approaches to be followed in the outreach process and the linkages with institutions such as Jan Shiksha Sansthan, and Krishi Vigyan Kendra have also been outlined in this paper.

Gandhigram University is one of the oldest and pioneering rural universities in (TN), India which accords the highest priority for rural outreach programmes. Typologising the activities, Boraian lists institute-based, department-based and student-based activities which encompass technology transfer, surveys and studies, awareness programmes, health camps, leadership and skill training, forming community based organisations, teaching rural children and providing resource support. Enumerating the problems encountered in the process of outreach, the work highlights various suggestions for effective rural outreach which include allocation of one fourth of a university's grant towards rural outreach programmes.

Outreach by Colleges

Integrated Village Development Programme (IVDP) by Agriculture College and Research Institute, Tamil Nadu Agriculture University is an innovative institutional linkage programme for village development says Mahendrakumar. The programme banked upon providing technical know how and enabling convergence of appropriate government departments. However, experience revealed that the farmers could not be reached only through technical know how but required more tangible resources. Linkage of several other institutions related to the rural sector proved risky due to lack of coordination, untimely coverage, delay in conducting meetings and non-cooperation from farmers.

Child Centered Outreach

The seminar focused, among other things, on reaching out to rural children. Suriakanthi argues that children need not be merely the beneficiaries, but can also be change agents themselves. Receiving knowledge, information and skills from resource persons, the children under a "Child to Child Project," shared it with their peer groups, more effectively than adults. Besides educating their fellow children, the children also started educating the community and parents, besides taking good care of their younger siblings at home.

Non-Government Organisations often intervene in situations where social conditions have deteriorated and the available resources cannot bring out lasting positive changes. Instead of trying to cure the social crises, Rajkumar says that we need to build a society capable of preventing these breakdowns altogether. This can better be accomplished by children, who are the future decision makers. After conceptualising children's participation, facilitation of children's participatory project and explaining organisational culture and corporate requirements, he provides the myth and reality of child participation.

Citing National Policy on Education (1986) which says that the consciousness of environment must permeate all ages and all sections of society beginning with the child, Bhanumathi describes the approaches to environmental education and outlines the role of rural school teachers in conducting awareness programmes, skill development activities, and formation of Eco-clubs among the students in schools. Participation of rural children in these activities encourages children to take up larger issues at a later stage in their lives, asserts the author.

Extension work is a fertile ground for experimentation of students' knowledge, skills and expertise in their field, argues Kavitha @ Maithily. She depicts her experiments through students in a service village of Home Science department which include education of school children through entertainment, magic shows, nutrition demonstrations, learning through natural colour extraction, summer joy programmes and community services. She argues that children could be reached out effectively through the above strategies which would act as a major tool to develop sensitivity among the students and build them up as social engineers.

Women and Youth

Agricultural programmes are often planned by men and mechanisation resulted in retaining the burden of women, if not increase it further, notes Sakuntalai. After establishment of Centre for Soil Salinity Research and implementation of TANWA (Tamil Nadu Women in Agriculture Programme), women underwent transformation in their social and economic lives. The author made case studies on the level of women empowerment and their influence on the group and community in general. It highlights how the process of outreach and the inputs and interventions by development organisations and programmes impacted on the tribal women.

Arguing NSS is the largest community outreach system in the country, Rajalakshmi outlines the methodology and objectives of NSS camps by girl students of Sri Avinashilingam University. The criteria used while planning special camps, and the areas covered under such camps, which include awareness campaign, skill training programme, and asset creation are discussed. It also highlights the dimensions, analyses the constraints, and formulates suitable recommendations for designing outreach programmes through NSS in the context of a women's university.

Balasubramaniyan describes the role of a Government institution *viz.*, Institute of People's Education (i.e Jan Shikshan Sansthan - JSS) under Ministry of Human Resource Development, Government of India in reaching out to the literate unemployed youth. Through short skill training programmes – both theory and practical – JSS has transformed the economic lives of young men and women from villages and towns. It outlines the content of these programmes, their delivery to the target groups and how they have benefited men and women through success stories.

Outreach in Kerala State

Rajagiri, a pioneering social work college in Kerala, focuses on a number of interventions in addressing the problems confronting the communities around, say Binoy Joseph and Antoni. Child-centered programmes, family-based rehabilitation programmes for senior citizens through its LIVE LABS, *Kudumbashree* programme, Sanitation programme, Solar electrification project, Community development, Women empowerment, Environment, Health and reformative activities such as legal aid, education and peace are listed out in the paper as the major rural outreach activities of Rajagiri College of Social Sciences.

An effective two way information flow between the small rubber production farmers and Field Officers who function as the 'eyes and ears' of the Rubber Board, facilitated the diffusion of updated farm science to the farming community. With feed back on problems from the farm, the scientists were able to find apt solution for rubber production, notes Usha Rani. Gradually, the priority shifted from a 'tree-centered' approach to 'man-centered' approach and the community assumed a core position. Subsequently, the Board introduced a 'participatory extension management system' through formation of Rubber Producers' Societies which were registered as the Village level Associations of Small holders. This unique outreach strategy was found to be successful among small rubber producers. It highlights certain distinct outreach values useful to outreach workers.

Sreekantan Thampi proposes a low or no cost outreach model for rural development based on a village development experiment in Kerala State. Instead of financial resources, information and technology were taken to the masses. Opportunities, motivation and volunteering proved more vital than material and financial resources. Projects that could generate sustainable life patterns, locations that could help in mending lives of people with average means, and organised and group activities that could tender successful results are portrayed in this work. After describing a series of projects and practices, he throws light on the factors which contributed to the success of activities at zero cost.

Experiments in Rural Outreach

Most of the rural extension programmes by college students turn out to be a one shot affair with a 'hit and go' approach, laments Boraian and feels that programmes which have a long-term vision and lasting benefits to the community, with an in-built component of sustainability, are the need of the hour. Precisely with these components, he outlines an innovative Micro Soft Programme i.e., micro level solution oriented field training programme, which has already been tested out in the field by Master's students of Gandhigram University.

Diabetes mellitus, once a wealthy man's affliction has now spread to all levels of society. The bad news is that it is increasing but the good news is that it can be prevented or at worst delayed even with simple, easy and effective steps like lifestyle modifications, says Padmini Balagopal. She describes the process and impact of a diabetes prevention research study and an intervention project through nutrition demonstration in a service village near Gandhigram, carried out by the Dept. of Home Science through a sponsored project from AAPI, USA. This study showed that a focused, intensive and culturally relevant education programme is effective not only in significantly reducing blood glucose level but also in improving their nutritional intake.

Manikandan and Eswaran depict the process of organising a three months training programme for Self Help Group women, its management, outcome and the lessons learnt. The programme centered around participatory approaches and methods, with semi-structured training design. In the process, it shifted the emphasis from authoritian to democratic approaches, centralisation to decentralised management and theoretical knowledge to practical application of the learning in field. This work analyses as to how a training programme can become a means of outreach to the self-help group women.

Supported by the various Government departments and financial institutions, women belonging to SHGs promoted by Gandhigram Trust (an NGO), gained financial independence, administrative experience and got relieved from the clutches of money lenders, notes Krishnaswamy. His work highlights how a new marketing strategy designed by the NGO has successfully enabled the select women SHG members to strengthen their economic status and empower them.

Technology Outreach

The latest advances in Information Technology (IT), computers, telecommunications and Internet have provided a conducive environment for adopting new technologies and making the method of instructions more effective and interactive, observe Nirmala and Sekhar. Internet has become an unavoidable necessity for organisations especially those involved in technology transfer. Internet and its application are also very useful in agricultural research, education, extension, planning of crop production, forecasting, post-harvest management, marketing, disaster management, etc. Such an application of internet would ensure proper growth of the agricultural sector on a sustainable basis, it claims.

Central and State Governments are increasingly turning to watershed approach as a means of achieving greater results from their area development programmes because, managing area development programmes on a watershed basis makes good sense – environmentally, financially and socially, says Mani. Outlining the various problems in using watershed approach to reach out to people, it proposes suitable remedies related to administration, awareness creation and capacity building, people's participation, user groups, self help groups, principal implementing agency and NGOs.

While the farming community is catered to by Agricultural Universities, farmers with livestock are served by the Veterinary University (TANUVAS), say Mathialagan and Manivannan. Training of youth and women on livestock management, establishing livestock and fisheries enterprises, providing advisory services and dissemination of livestock related technology are promoted through training, consultation, meeting, demonstration, distances education, radio, television, newspaper and publications.

Wrap Up

Contributed by professionals, both development practitioners and the Faculty from colleges and universities in Tamil Nadu, Karnataka and Kerala shed light on the various dimensions and dilemmas facing the process of reaching out to the rural community – women, children, youth, farmers, self help groups, tribals and so on. These work focus on the criticality of outreach in the process of rural development.

Outreach programmes succeed or fail for various reasons. Primary among them are the outreach agency, the clientele community, the outreach process, the setting of the community and the external environment. Regarding the outreach agency, their basic philosophy of outreach, experience in outreach, resource and technology endowment, design and content of their outreach programmes, approaches, strategies and methods of outreach mattered the most. In respect of the clientele community, their socio-cultural milieu, backwardness, level of literacy, perception of outreach, and expectation from the outreach agency may be considered critical.

Scheduling of outreach programmes, distance to the community, mode of reaching the target groups, cost involved, quality of outreach workers and method of executing the programme impinge upon the process of outreach. Geographic location of the habitations of the target community, its physiological and geological features, the flora and fauna, climate and rainfall, farming systems, livelihood base of the community and the vagaries of nature determine the character of the outreach setting. External environment such as policies and programmes of the government, legislations, business environment, and political support exert their influence on the outreach programmes and their impact.

On the whole, it may be stated that wherever outreach was a necessity and formed an essential adjunct of the agencies' central programmes, it tended to be more successful, as against outreach agencies where it was only an option and a fascination.

Chapter 2

Community Outreach Methodologies– The Canvas of Concepts

M.P. Boraian

Concept of Outreach

'Community' refers to a group of people living in a particular local area such as a hamlet, village or a settlement, or the body of people in a learned occupation such as those in business, health profession or legal profession. In biotic sense, a community, as an ecological unit, may refer to a group of interdependent organisers inhabiting the same region and interacting with each other. In sociological sense, community refers to a group of people having ethnic or cultural or religious characteristics in common, or those having a community of harmonious interests. The concept of community is integral and all encompassing and hence it assumes significance in the geographic, occupational, biotic, as well as sociological sense.

'Outreach' is defined as an act or a process of reaching beyond, the act of reaching out. It is an effort to build connections from one person to another or one group to another or the extension of assistance or services to persons or groups not previously served. It is described as an effort by an organisation or group to connect its ideas or practices to the efforts of the other organisations, groups or specific audience or the general public. It is a systematic attempt to provide service beyond conventional limits, to particular segments of a community.

Outreach often targets a neglected population, lacking in certain vital needs and deserving external intervention. According to Harnoll (1990), outreach is "a community oriented activity, undertaken in order to contact individuals or groups from particular target populations, who are not effectively contacted or reached by existing services or though traditional...... channels."

Outreach interventions are more flexible, need based, and rarely rigid; they are either sectoral or comprehensive. Outreach work is often underpinned by an ethos of community development and empowerment, developing coalitions between workers, clients, their peers and families. There is often no set or standard intervention, but rather a commitment to responding to issues by the target group in a wholistic way (EMCDDA, 2000). "Outreach can be hard to define, but usually refers to activities designed to make contact with clients primarily in their natural settings (EMCDDA, 1999). These activities can be delivered by professionals or peers."

Certain institutions have outreach as their 'mission', either by deliberate choice or as 'mandated' by the state. Outreach is also considered as a 'programme' structured after the primary concerns of the respective change agents, and recognised as an 'activity' under each programme. As a 'process', it conceives, structurises and channelises the ideas and inputs from change agents into backward communities and brings about transformation in their social and economic lives.

Outreach by a change agent also serves as a 'method' of social work, for it brings together individuals and institutions intending to serve the community, through an intervention mechanism. As a 'means', outreach is used as a conduit of disseminating development ideas, sharing developmental inputs or undertake development interventions.

Outreach is an opportunity for change agents and a necessity for the needy communities. With basic commitment for community service, the change agents often partner with their clients and contribute to the removal of their backwardness and ushering in prosperity. Community outreach may therefore be defined "as a mission or mandate, a programme or process, and method or means, deliberately designed by change agents in order to solve the basic problems of a group or community through a multitude of approaches, strategies and methods in the socio-cultural setting of the target population."

Outreach by Universities

Outreach has been pursued by a plethora of change agents – funding agencies, public sector undertakings, banks, corporates, hospitals, colleges and universities, and many other institutions. Funding agencies, besides their primary responsibilities of project appraisal, approval, monitoring and evaluation, also undertake direct intervention projects in the target communities. Similarly, banks, corporates and public sector undertakings (PSU) undertake outreach programmes in their neighbourhood communities, as part of their Corporate Social Responsibility (CSR). Hospitals carry out health based outreach activities, in the respective areas of specialisation, with service motive. Colleges and universities have twin objectives of helping the community and in the process, train their students. The outreach programmes of universities, therefore differ from their counterparts both in content and delivery. Many universities across the globe have separate units, departments or divisions for outreach.

Universities overseas have the tripartite division of teaching, research and service. Outreach has been traditionally identified with "service". Outreach covers the full spectrum of knowledge functions – generating knowledge, transmitting, applying and preserving knowledge. When scholars generate knowledge, they discover or create it: when they transmit knowledge, they share it with others; and when they apply knowledge, they help others to address circumstances and problems. Outreach has therefore the same potential for scholarship as the other major academic functions of the university such as teaching and research.

Outreach has traditionally been considered as a service activity. Outreach activities provide benefit to the community as academy. A community may receive valuable consultation from a faculty member that may help them solve a water contamination problem, while the faculty member obtains valuable insights about contamination that help shape plans for a subsequent research project. In order for a faculty to solve a problem confronting the community, the inputs required are basic theoretical knowledge as the foundation, current research on the subject matter and a service bent to benefit the community.

'Outreach' describes the various ways in which the university extends it expertise for the direct benefit of local communities and other external audience. The faculty has core responsibilities of teaching, research and creative work, and service on campus. Outreach can be an important and valued aspect of these responsibilities.

Outreach is a form of scholarship that cuts across teaching, research and service. It involves generating, transmitting, applying and preserving knowledge for the direct benefits of external audiences in ways that are consistent with university and unit missions. When they do these things for the direct benefit of external audiences, they are doing university outreach.

Outreach vs Extension

Universities in India, primarily concentrate on teaching, research and extension activities. Extension, though an important component, is not an independent component; instead, it is an amalgam of both teaching and research. Outreach and extension are not exclusive to each other. Instead, they are more inclusive and integral. In as much as they have similarities of approaches, strategies, methods and techniques, they do possess certain distinct characteristics.

Outreach encompasses a broad range of activities designed by designated units or departments of universities in pursuit of community service. Faculty, staff and students involve themselves in the outreach process, using a multitude of methods, reaching a select group or the whole community. Needs of the group or community, resources available with the outreach unit, package of methodologies practiced and participation by the community determine the shape and size of their outreach programmes. Providing literacy to illiterates in rural areas, organising health camp for tribals in hill areas or facilitating disabled persons to avail welfare programmes may form part of outreach.

On the other hand, extension focuses upon dissemination of knowledge and ideas based on the recent advancements in science and technology, to those people who need to use it most. Extension has a specific message, uses select methods, has distinct target groups and aims at bringing about concrete changes in the knowledge, attitude and behaviour of people. Agricultural scientists educating farmers on drip irrigation or Nutrition experts demonstrating supplementary nutrition to women and children, Veterinary scientists propagating hybrid animals among the cattle owners may form part of extension activities. Similarities and differences apart, both 'outreach' and 'extension' activities benefit the communities around and aim at promoting their welfare which forms part of the social responsibilities of every public university.

Extension, Outreach and Engagement

Similar to the concept of 'extension' used in Indian universities, 'engagement' is used in foreign universities, as most akin to outreach. Engagement means partnering in the local, state-wide or national or international communities, and not simply extending what you know to some one else, who presumably does not know.

Extension, outreach and engagement are almost synonymous in meaning. Engagement, emphasises mutual respect, collaboration, power sharing, reciprocity, partnerships in which the university and a public (a client group) collaborate in sharing knowledge, embracing common goals, and in mounting action to respond to or to resolve an issue/problem. The function of extension, outreach/engagement is embedded in the university's mission and is on an equal par with the other two functions namely; teaching and research.

The focus of university extension/outreach/engagement is to engage the university in planning for and facilitating change in its external publics, as defined by the university's mission. The conceptual framework will emphasise knowing the external environment of the university, identify the leaders of each of these publics and their stakeholders, partnering with these leaders in collaborative needs identification, assessment and analysis, designing and implementing joint programmes to respond to these assessed needs, and importantly, measuring outcomes achieved and demonstrating accountability with respect to the planned programmes.

Outreach 'engages' the university with the community in economic, social, cultural, environmental and educational issues. It applies the teaching, research, and knowledge resources of the university to benefit the public throughout the world. Outreach takes an educational component (i.e. the dissemination of ideas) but it is increasingly common for organisations to conceive their outreach strategies as a two way street in which Outreach is framed as 'engagement' rather than solely on dissemination or education.

Typology of Outreach

Outreach is better conceived as a cross-cutting function. There are forms of outreach teaching, research, service and consulting, just as there are forms of non-outreach teaching, research, service and consulting.

Under teaching outreach, the faculty members extend their expertise to the external community. When the Faculty teach courses to non-traditional students off-campus, or conduct seminars workshops, consultation or technical assistance, it forms part of teaching outreach. Outreach in education includes using teaching or demonstration skills in an area of expertise to shape intentionally the potential of individuals or groups outside the college community. Outreach in education may affect others' intellectual, creative, or problem-solving skills and includes technology transfer, policy review, and other events involving information dissemination between the college and outside audiences. For example, teaching a traditional resident class is education; teaching a customised programme through the Centre for Adult Learning is outreach.

Under Research outreach, the faculty conduct research intended to respond to pressing problems or issues identified by external constituencies such as local communities, state, national or international agencies, business, schools, hospitals or other public non-profit organisations. Outreach in research includes intellectual, creative, and problem-solving interactions between the college and external constituencies. This includes technology transfer, policy review, and other events involving information discovery and/or disseminating the results of the discovery between the college and outside audiences. For example, completing a funded research project and publishing a paper related to international banking is research; hosting a workshop for the financial community to disseminate the results is outreach.

Service outreach takes place when the students or faculty from a unit of college or a university extends service to the external constituencies through programmes or activities with an outreach component. Outreach in service includes service to communities, governments, corporations, professional organisations, learned societies, and other external constituencies. Activities may include task forces, public hearings, professional performances, and other events that are based on the expertise of the faculty member(s) involved. For example, forming an association of Disabled students on the college campus is service; enabling the disabled in the rural vicinity to access welfare programmes of government is outreach.

Consulting is considered as another form of outreach. Faculty and staff members routinely make knowledge available to the public, private and non-profit sectors in the form of consulting. Consulting requires scholarly expertise and frequently involves creating, transmitting, applying and/or preserving knowledge for the direct benefit of external audiences. When the faculty offers consultancy on development intervention efforts benefiting the rural communities around, it may be considered as a form of consultancy outreach.

Contributions to University

Besides its contribution to surrounding society, outreach also makes three important contributions to the university itself :

Vitality in Research and Training: Outreach affords faculty, staff and students windows on current reality, and the perspectives gained through these windows inform a scholar's understanding of the contemporary meaning, value, and use of their disciplinary or professional knowledge. It also raises important and fascinating questions.

Institutional identity: Even when outreach is restricted to solving problems with existing knowledge, it often inspires new research, thereby enriching and guiding the scholarly work of the university.

Political and financial viability: Recognition of the university as a source of usable knowledge across many domains has strong appeal for public, private, profit and non-profit institutions, state and local governments and individual citizens. Outreach helps create an explicit link between the university and large society on which it depends for legitimacies and support.

Dimensions of Outreach

The university reaches out to external audiences in one or more of these dimensions: distance, time and place, and format and approach. It attends itself

- in *distance,* when it makes its knowledge resources accessible to those who do not live nearby
- in *time* and *place,* when knowledge resources are made available at convenient times and location and
- in *format* and *approach,* when knowledge is made available in ways that are appropriate for those who seek it.

Facets of Outreach

When a school, college or university or any of their constituent units is organising outreach programmes in the community around, they may develop a plan to provide outreach engagement with focus on answering the following questions :

Focus/Target group: Does the plan include a means to assess community interests or needs? Does the unit have a clear understanding that community members (i.e. children/adults, local or statewide) would be served by the plan and is the plan evaluated?

In-built assessment: Does the unit include assessments in its outreach /engagement plan development?

Type of activities: Are the engagement activities one-way (i.e. news letters) or two-way (Public meeting with Question - Answer)?

Time: What amount of time is dedicated to outreach/engagement daily? Is this appropriate for the nature of the unit?

Person(s) responsible: Who is responsible for the outreach/engagement activities?

Faculty commitment: Do Faculty workloads reflect this level of commitment?

Method of evaluation: Is there a method to evaluate these activities? Does the outreach/engagement plan change in response to evaluation? i.e. an Engagement table that summarises workload and outcomes for individual school and / or units.

Outreach Log

An outreach log is a document that lists information about outreach contact. It usually lists when outreach was conducted, who was contacted, the type of contact, purpose of contact, materials distributed, and the outcome of the contact. (See Table 1 for a sample Outreach log.)

The outreach log should include the following:

- date of contact,
- name of staff making contact,
- name, address, and telephone number of the organisation contacted,
- type of contact (for example, "telephone contact", "visit", "correspondence", "posters", newsletter", etc.)
- purpose of contact (for example, "to request referrals", "to provide information", "public service announcement", etc.)
- materials provided, and outcome.

Wrap Up

Outreach is thus a process of planned intervention to mitigate the sufferings of neighbouhood communities, and scale up their resource potential, vigorously pursued by a plethora of change agents. Important among them are universities and colleges, who practice varied forms of outreach-teaching outreach, research outreach, service outreach and outreach through consultancy. Outreach process has a multitude of dimensions and facets which are to be considered by outreach workers while designing outreach programmes. An outreach log could be a handy tool in assisting them in their outreach mission.

The author has drawn from the Outreach experiences of select universities in United States viz., University of Alaska, Colorado, Massachusetts, Pennsylvania and Rhode Islands, besides California Department of Health Services in the preparation of this work. The author gratefully acknowledges all these sources. More details can be had from the following websites:

www.wicworks.ca.gov/

www.msu.edu./

www.alaska.edu/

www.colorado.edu/

www.umass.edu/outreach

www.uri.edu/

www.princeton.edu/

www.pennstate.behrend.psu.edu/

Table 1
Outreach Log

	Name of Staff / Designation	Contact Person / Organization	Type of Contact	Purpose of Contact	Activity	Outcome
20/08/07	Outreach staff team	Tribal people	Visit to tribal area	Identification of problems	• Organize people, through local leaders • Discuss with them • Identify their problems	1. Rapport established with people 2. List of problems elicited 3. Representatives selected
21/08/07	Outreach Coordinator /Tribal Representatives	District Collector	Visit to Collector office	Redressal of grievances	• Briefing problems, with background information • Submission of petition • Appeal for early intervention	• Officials sensitized on tribal issues • Concern generated for early action
22/08/07	Outreach Coordinator / Tribal Representatives	Project officer, DRDA	Visit to DRDA office	Regarding grant for housing	• Hardships in dwelling explained • List of Beneficiaries submitted • House building assistance sought	• Magnitude of the problem presented • Application considered favorably.
23/08/07	Outreach Coordinator / Tribal Representatives	Block development Officer	Letter	Regarding drinking water problem	• Representation got signed by the members of tribal community • Request letter submitted • Early solution requested	• Nature of hardships explained • Officials promised to visit the settlement.

Contd. . .

Contd. . .

24/08/07	Outreach Team / Tribal Representatives	Village Panchayat President	Personal visit	Regarding street light	• Hardship faced by women explained • Representation submitted	• Electricity officials contacted • Early action promised
25/08/07	Outreach Team / Tribal Representatives	Head of local voluntary agency	Phone call	Regarding Balwadi for children	• Profile of children submitted • Problems highlighted	• Resources mobilized • People's cooperation for a rent free building sought. • Local teacher identified
26/08/07	Outreach Coordinator / Tribal Representatives	Bank Manager	Personal visit	Regarding application for loan	• Filled up loan forms submitted • Beneficiaries introduced to Bank Manager	• Applications processed • Recommendations made for sanction.

Chapter 3

Community Outreach Methodologies: Concepts and Technicalities

R. Mohanraj

Definition of Outreach

The working definition of Outreach has undergone a change, corresponding to the change in approach to development. In the traditional welfarist approach, Outreach has the working definition in terms of compassion and sympathy. It is one reaching out to a less fortunate, as a manifestation of concern and doing good. The definition was based on the principles of *dharma*. Even a person offering a friendly cup of tea to his neighbour would come under the concept of Outreach. The definition included any act of concern of one for the other beyond oneself. This applied to individuals, families, religious and academic institutions. Under this definition, the intentions mattered more than the effect. The gesture was the indicator. What was being given was not important but the intention by the giver to the receiver is what mattered.

With the change of development approach from welfarism into participation and self-help, the definition also changed. The change was in the reference for the definition. It changed from *dharma* to performance. The definition took its reference from the physical science, which advocates the concept of reach in terms of input and output. All physical activities have an equation of input and output governing them. For example, an adult who has an intake of 1200 calories per day can deliver the output of walking at the rate of six kilometres per hour. This is the input – output equation of the walker; or what is called the 'reach' of the walker. When the walker does beyond the rate of six kilometres per hour, he is extending the equation; or, in other words 'Out reaching'.

In situations where development is associated with performance, Outreach is treated as a performance term. It is related to situations expressing excellence or extra ordinary or beyond the target in input – output equation. It also includes doing things differently which can establish the outreach in input and output.

Development is a social science. The context for development is governed by *cause – effect* equations. For example, poverty which is one of the key agendas of social development has a matrix of class/caste and gender causes and its effect in the form of economic and non-economic deprivation on sections of society. Interventions based on *means–end* connectivity enables the impact on the developmental context. Means in the form of economic/ social/cultural and political interventions for these deprived sections of society ends their situation of poverty. The *means–end* connectivity for the context in development is established through the process of *Input–Output–Impact (IOI)*. For example, for a person below poverty line, inputs in the form of skills, motivation and capital leads to the output of increase in income and the impact of the person crossing the poverty line.

The working definition of outreach links up to the context of self-reliance and sustainability in development. Outreach becomes applicable when the input is cost and energy efficient, delivering an input, which has elements of spread effect, self-reliance, growth through self-reliance, which is the basic constituent for sustainability and replicability.

Intervention through Extension and Outreach

In development interaction between the promoter and the stakeholder is the fundamental process. There are two categories of promoters in this interaction. The first category consists of an individual, a religious or academic institution, corporates with social accountability and institutions of the mainstream sector such as Banks. The primary mission and purpose of these identities is something else. But they have a concern for the people below poverty line and express this concern in the form of an action. For example, an individual who has concern for his neighborhood or village expresses this concern in the form of activities such as planting trees or cleaning his neighborhood. Religious institutions may provide free educational opportunities for the children of deprived sections of society in the educational institutions run by them.

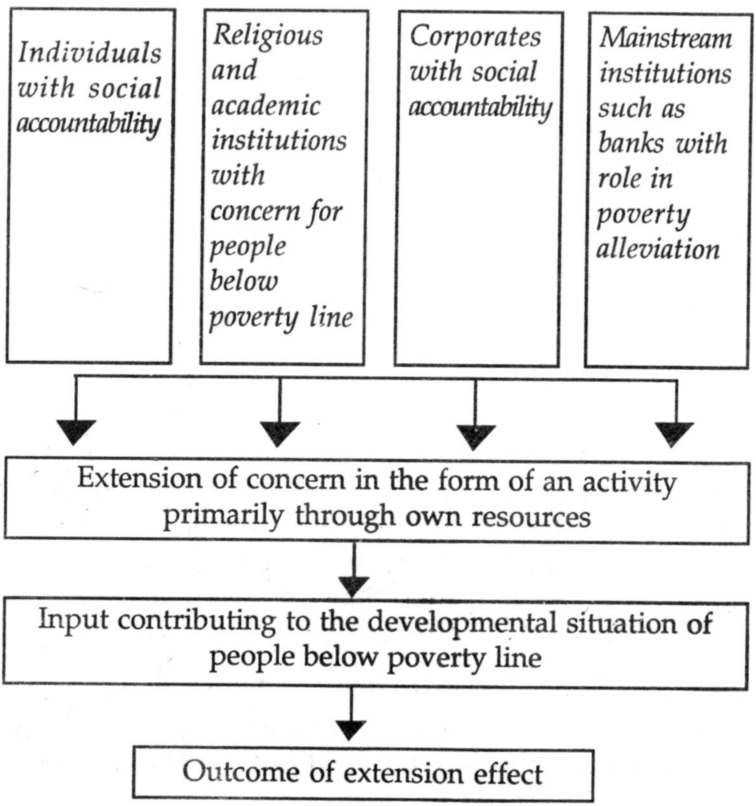

Academic institutions may express their concern for villages by organising games and sports activity for the children in the village through their student extension program. Corporates take projects on employment opportunity by setting up ancillary production units in communities. Banks express their concern for the villages by adopting villages for providing credit for the people in it. For these involvements, these players predominantly use their own resources and supplement their resources from other sources, primarily through networking as found necessary. These players extend their concern for the people who are below poverty line in the form of an activity.

The second is the Non-Governmental Development Organizations (NGDO) whose main mission is development work. Their stated mission is to work for and work with the deprived and disadvantaged in society who are the primary stakeholders in development. They do this in collaboration with Government and resource organisations in the North. They access development projects from their Governmental and non-Governmental resource partners to implement development projects for the stakeholder.

Traditionally, what the first category adopted was an extension approach to development. The extension approach was input oriented with a logical outcome of the impact contributing to the development of the people below poverty line. The NGDOs adopted an outreach approach. Under outreach approach, the methodology involved a planned input – output and impact (IOI) sequence. There were different levels of performance in the outreach approach. While most of them stayed with the extension of input orientedness, a small proportion could monitor the IOI equation and establish the outreach effect.

Over the past years, there is a trend towards the first category of players joining the NGDOs in adopting outreach approach through implementation of projects of multiple forms and profiles. While some are conscious about the distinction between extension and outreach many others continue what they are doing under the name of outreach. The consequence is varied.

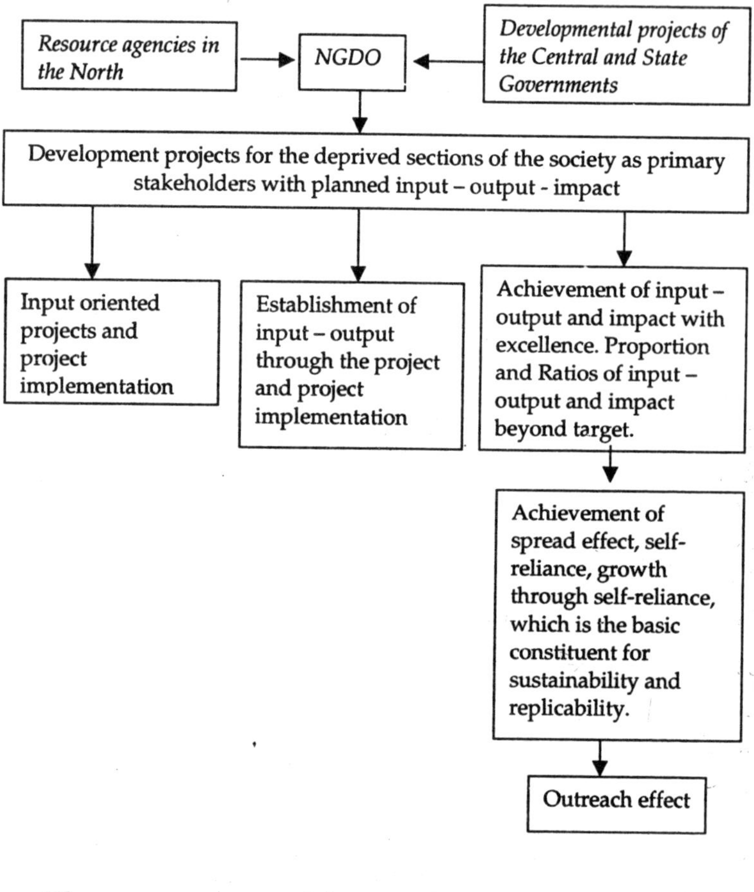

The corporates with social accountability have formalised their community development through appropriate systems, policies and procedures. Many corporates have their community development departments with formulated policies for community development, clarity on their stakeholders, community development projects with defined IOI and the strategies to implement the projects.

- The mainstream institutions such as Banks have linked up with the government in specific areas such as credit, capacity building and livelihood strengthening. Through this, they have been able to establish their IOI equations and continue to work based on it. While some have confined themselves to credit for the Self help groups (SHGs), many others have developed projects on training and capacity building with specificity, measurability, attainability, replicability and time boundedness (SMART).
- A good number of individuals with social accountability have expanded themselves into base level Community based Organisations (CBOs) under the provisions of SHGs.
- Most of the religious institutions have taken a dual path. **1.** Integration of their extension activities into the provision of SHGs. **2.** To retain the activities related to faith and belief system such as *bajana mandalis*, to retain them in their autonomy and individual identity.
- In the case of academic institutions, while they have been progression in the structural aspects, the programme areas require review and strengthening. On the structural side, identities such as NSS provide good support to the student community for their involvement in extension work. But in the anxiety of the academic institutions in their change over from extension to outreach the student community, which is the primary stakeholder of the academic institutions, are overstretched with commitment for outreach. The consequence is double ended. At the end of the student community, the boundaries between the primary objective of excellence in their studentship and their accountability for community development is vague. At the end of the communities, it is high level of input orientedness which does not match the expectations of the stakeholders, who desire definite change in the quality of their lives through planned IOI.

Technicalities to Deliver Outreach Effect

The technicalities involved in delivering the outreach effect through projects are as follows:

Promoter – stakeholder relationship

The form of relationship between the promoter and stakeholder is a crucial contribute or determining the outreach effect.

Promoter - - - - - - - - - Stakeholder

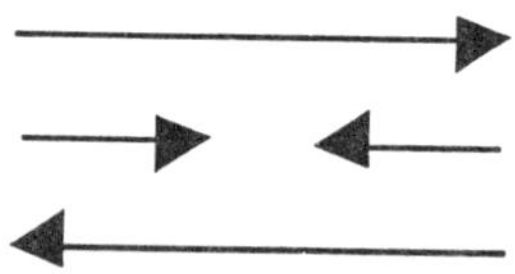

There are three types of relationship between the promoter and stakeholder.

- One is the promoter-driven relationship. In this relationship, the promoter thinks and decides for the stakeholder and designs the project. The stakeholder is brought in at the stage of implementation. The choice of a fairly good proportion of NGOs for tailoring training for women would be an example for this. This relationship could be because of the welfarist approach based on the assumption of '0 level awareness and knowledge of the stakeholder'. In this relationship, the promoter assumes that the stakeholder is poor due to lack of awareness and knowledge. The method of interaction between the promoter and stakeholder is based on the 'banking method'. The mode of input is predominantly in the form of 'telling them what they need to do'. This relationship is also perpetuated because of the type of projects available for implementation for the NGDO from the resource agencies in the North and Government.
- The second is a partner relationship in which the promoter and stakeholder work together as partners

in designing the project. The approach is one of equity relationships between the two. An example of this would be the project working with a group of farmers to increase their agricultural productivity. In this, the promoter listens to the experiences of the farmers, does the needs assessment through them, identifies the different options and designs the option of short variety pulse as the strategy for improving agricultural productivity through joint decision of the promoter and stakeholder. In the project implementation, there is role division between the promoter and stakeholder. The planning, monitoring and evaluation of the project is done jointly by both. This relationship is based on the acknowledgement of the awareness and knowledge of the stakeholder. Interaction between the promoter and stakeholder is based on shared learning principle. Inputs are in the form of adult learning and experiential learning methodologies. In this relationship, the promoter and stakeholder acknowledge the strength in them and bring it to a constructive collaboration based on negotiation on roles and accountability on agreed activities.

- The third is a stakeholder-driven relationship. This could be positive, such as a group of farmers in a drought area who are in need of doing something with a promoter to sustain their livelihood. In this case, the relationship is based on mutual trust between the promoter and the stakeholder. Besides trust, the second element that sustains this relationship is the technical and social expertise of the promoter to nurture the basic trust of the stakeholder into a partner relationship described above. Or it could be negative such as the milk cooperative started by a NGO under the pressure of a group of local politicians and their relatives! This happens due to reasons such as weakness and lack of professionalism in the promoter as an organisation, pressure of project implementation and performance by the resource partners, undefined stakeholder constituency and poor community contact between the promoter and the stakeholder.

Project form and implementation methodology

- The directional relationship between the two players determines the project form and its implementation methodology. The promoter-driven relationship invariably adopts Project Cycle Methodology (PCM). In PCM, the initiative begins with promoter. The promoter decides the project and plans its implementation over a long period. The stakeholder cooperates with the promoter to implement the project according to the stated IOI. The project is in three phases: 1. Formation. 2. Formalisation and 3. Consolidation. The project period stretches over 7-9 years. Ownership and continuation responsibility of the project effect is the key focus of the consolidation phase. The developmental projects implemented during the 1960s and upto the mid-70s were predominantly based on welfarist model. The model is based on the perception of '0 level knowledge and capability of the stakeholder'.
- The second model is the Project Cycle Methodology (PCM) with a higher level of participation but based on same components such as long term of 7-9 years and input orientedness. The difference comes in components such as division of roles between the promoter and stakeholder and change of inputs based on monitoring. Based on a scale of participation, the project has provisions for and the role transition between the promoter and stakeholder during the project period. The stakeholder is involved in the accountability for *IOI*. This is called developmental partnership model. The development projects during mid-1970s to end-80s adopted this model in good proportions.

The third model is stakeholder-centered. Here, the initiative begins from the stakeholder or the stakeholder is enabled to identify their developmental needs, prioritise and identify interventions to address the priorities. Besides identifying the context for development, the stakeholder is helped to undertake the initiative to formulate the *IOI* and the project framework to carry the *IOI*. The role of the promoter is to enable the structuring of this initiative through functions such as objective setting, systems development, strategic planning and resource planning. This is called the accompaniment model.

The specific character of this model is that it is short time based. It involves negotiation with the stakeholder. The ownership and accountability for the initiative rests with the stakeholder from day one. The model is credit based and built on establishing sustainability through self-management and recycling of the money involved in the project. The model is based on the concept of self-help. This model became prominent in the Government during the 1990s with the concept of 'self help' as the key strategy for development.

The second set of players who adopt the model in high proportion are the corporates with social accountability and mainstream institutions such as banks with role in poverty alleviation. The model, which has the maximum scope to deliver the outreach effect, has an inbuilt contradiction with the profile of the conventional NGDOs who are linked to resource agencies in the North who raise money for spending on projects in the South through NGDO projects. This model, in a nutshell, can be called as the feasible formula for achieving the outreach effect. For practicality, this work defines this model as the outreach model.

The outreach model components can be defined as follows:

Structure	Systems	Process	Approach
1. Organisational relationship between the promoter and stakeholder as partners in designing and implementing the development project based on common minimal understanding. 2. Networking with Government and non-Government organisational identities with compatible ideology and approach on issues and developmental activities. 3.Organisational renewal with time and change.	1. Promote and strengthen appropriate systems for the organisation of the stakeholder (CBO). Capacity building for the functional-zing of the systems to the level of self-management and optimal efficiency. 2. Systems for basic management such as organisational management, Communication, PME (planning, monitoring and evaluation), resource mobilisation. 3.Horizon scanning, acknowledgement of time and change and systems and capacity building to cope with T &C	1.Ownership and accountability with the CBO. 2.Role division and transition between the promoter and CBO 3.Accountability for process and results. 4.Indicators and measurable (qualitative and quantitative) 5.Cross cutting themes such as mainstreaming gender and disability 6.Principle of equity, democracy and governance 7. Principle of building on strengths and potentials. 8. Monitoring of the Input: Output: Impact ratio (IOI) 9. Negotiation between the promoter and stakeholder on developmental agendas. 10. Maintaining the boundaries of the different players and secondary stakeholders in the process.	1. *'Doing things differently. Not doing different things'.* 2.Creativity 3.Innovation 4.Growth with self-reliance. Growth with no liability. 5.Stakeholder centeredness 6.Delegation 7.Networking 8.Learning from failures. Re - planning. Online action-reflection-action. 9. Integrated and holistic approach to the develop-ment context of the stake-holder. 10. Development through change and upgradation of attitudes and skills (Software and hardware component of development) 11. Awareness and base level organization to be the functional responsibility of the CBO. Not the promoter.

Profile of the Promoter and Stakeholder

The organisational profile of the Promoter is a primary factor in determining Outreach methodology. While the natural preference of Non- Governmental Development Organizations (NGDOs) uses Project Cycle Methodology, the preference of others such as corporate in community development and mainstream institutions such as Banks with role in poverty is for the Outreach methodology. This is mainly because while the exclusive mission of NGDOs is community development, for others their involvement in community development is a manifestation of their social accountability. Their main mission is something else. Academic institutions are in a crossroad situation. This is because of their effort to achieve the outreach effect through the student community whose primary mission is studentship with excellence.

At the side of the stakeholder, Community-based organisations with certain profile are more conducive for Outreach than others. For example, SHG or community-based economic organisations such as producer groups, cooperatives and economic activity collectives are more amenable to Outreach methodology than CBOs with political profiles. This is because while the former are more autonomous and operating on one or two specific agendas, the latter are invariably linked to other political alliances and operate on multiple agendas.

History of the context for development

In cases where the history and context for development is stakeholder-directed, the methodology is more towards outreach. Developmental context emerging out of crisis of livelihoods have more scope for Outreach. For example, the farmers in North Karnataka who are dependant on monsoon once in three years are more open to the model of outreach than the farmers in Tamil Nadu who desire more water for their third crop.

Resources and origin of resources

Projects with total dependency have much less option for outreach than those with a qualitative and quantitative amount of stakeholder contribution. NGDOs who are predominantly functional with donor support have the natural option of project cycle method, since the projects are long-term based and assured of donor support for the different phases of the project. Others such as corporate who invest their own funds have the natural option of maximum mileage for their money. The natural option of corporates with social accountability and mainstream institutions such as Banks with role in poverty alleviation is the Outreach methodology with components such as beneficiary contribution, ownership and accountability of the stakeholder, short-term and measurable impact.

Projects with priority for spread effect and replicability

- Projects have an inbuilt component of spiral effect and replicability towards continuation and sustainability of project impact. There are two options to achieve this component. One is the replicability of the project *per se* by the promoter. The project cycle model adopts this method for replicability and spread effect. For example, a project successfully implemented by a NGDO sets the track for a second donor to fund a similar project in a different geographical area. Or the same donor to extend the support to repeat the activity in another area or in the same area in a different form.

- The second is the replicability of the project effect and not the project. The Outreach model has the replicability of the project impact as a spread effect. The watershed development project being implemented in Padavedu in Tamil Nadu by TVS Sundaram Clayton is an example for this. The parent project is being implemented in 28 villages through the Water Users Association, a CBO promoted to be the partner organisation in the implementation of the project. The spread effect of the parent project is planned to be in the form of two other water and land development projects to be designed and implemented by the WUA.

Number of players: The dependency factor

When the player identity is confined to promoter and stakeholder, the option for outreach is higher. For example, in the case of corporates who are involved in community development, the player identity is confined to the promoter and stakeholder. Negotiations are direct. Role division is clear. Targets and indicators are measurable and specific. When there is a third intermediary, the preference is more for project cycle methodology. For example, donor-funded NGDOs have a higher preference for project cycle methodology. This is because of the necessity to accommodate the priorities of three players, align the priorities with macro trends of development and fit in the developmental priorities of the stakeholders into it.

Conclusion

Development is a social science, working on the key agenda of poverty alleviation. The two key players, the promoter and stakeholder, determine the process of development. The promoters in development are in two broad categories. **1.** The Non- Governmental Development Organizations (NGDO)s whose main mission is alleviation of poverty and are development alleviation of poverty promotion of development. **2.** Other main stream players such as academic institutions and corporate are involved in community development. These identities have their main mission and accommodate community development as a manifestation of their social accountability. Both these players in development have a variety of options on strategies and methodology.

Development has two key methodologies. One is the project cycle mode, which has characteristics such as long term, process orientedness and varying degrees of promoter

– stakeholder relationship in project designing and implementation. The other is the outreach mode, which has characteristics such as short term, result orientedness, and stakeholder-centered relationship.

Both the modes have their advantages and disadvantages. Developmental interventions choose the mode appropriate to them based on the concept, philosophy and practicalities related to the promoter.

References

1. Marion, E.Haynes., **Project Management: From ideas to implementation**, Crisp Publications Inc, Memlo Park, California.
2. Rajiv Shaw., **Surviving Tomorrow: Turn around strategies and perspectives in organisational design and development**, Vikas Publishing House Pvt. Ltd., Chennai.
3. Stephen, P. Osborne., **Managing in the Voluntary Sector: A Handbook for Managers in Charitable and Non Profit Organisations**, International Thompson Business Press, Delhi.
4. Chakravarthy, S.K., **Threshold of Motivation**, Tata Magram Hill, Delhi.
5. Mahesh,V.H., **Management by Values**, Oxford University Press, New Delhi.
6. Ken Mutejka & Richard, J Dunsingh., **A Manager's Guide to the Millennium**, Viva Books Pvt Ltd, Chennai.
7. Andrew Leigh, **Effective Change – 20 ways to make it happen**, Universities press, Hyderabad
8. Charles, W.L. Hill & Gareth, R. Jones., **Cases in Strategic Management (II Edition)**, Oxford University press, New Delhi.

Chapter 4

Community Outreach Methodologies

S. Alexander

Introduction

One of the most crucial interventions in the development of poor and marginalised is the outreach methodologies or strategies in the global contexts. In many cases of community based peoples' mobilisation, the basic result orientation is attributed to helping the community to be self assertive and self supportive. Consolidation of human resources as a basic requirement depend very much on the choice of suitable methodology in motivating the communities to realise specific goals in addressing their problems and issues.

The Outlook

People are vulnerable not only to problems, issues and exploitations but also to different types of development propositions as brought out to them for their own efforts and participation. Depending on different contexts in which they live, the change agents design strategies and methods of their outreach plans. Multinational and bilateral aid agencies are more structured in their approach and in many cases, their policies have a very strong methods relating to reaching out to the communities for various livelihood alternatives. Their support system / mission proposes a well disciplined development package delivery and to ensure impact envisaged in their proposal. Those aid recipients whether they are NGOs or other social organisations need to confine to such designs and the output of their service deliveries is mostly determined by efficient management of methods proposed for working with the communities.

There are donors who would like to grant freedom of choice to the recipient organisations but in this current decade, the general trend is to involve people for a participatory development approach. Awareness generation, maintaining the interest levels of the communities, decision making and actions related (AIDA model) to different interventions gain much importance in their working with the beneficiary communities.

Professionalisation in various development efforts has increased the need for efficiency in service delivery. Addressing basic issues and problems should recognise the efforts of people as collectives is considered to be one of the foundational requirements in working with communities in need.

Development policies undergo drastic changes with aid agencies time after time.

Outreaching methods

In many cases, the methods proposed are conditioned and confined to proper procedures to achieve results. For example, group building activities with particular focus on self help group methods have specific systems to be followed by both the service delivers and the subjects (people) of such methods. Community psychology proposes certain level of maturity on the part of people in functioning as groups, before implementing such programmes for their own development. Unfortunately, in several cases, important factors are not considered. Most of the self help group methodologies emphases economic empowerment as an important impact and the other factors such as environmental and ecological protection are ignored in the process. If the SHGs involved in farming, the ultimate aim is increasing production by using chemical inputs thereby causing damage to their environment and injustice to their own future generation. Shrimp culture is one example, for such degradations. The short term benefit is more income and money floating but the long term result is very much negative. In Bangladesh, the most successful experiments of SHGs are losing sight of such impact. Local resources and traditional practices are not altogether negative to be easily dismissed from our development plans for the people. In most of the Asian countries, we have already lost most valuable traditional practices in agriculture, seed and plant protection, preservation of forest wealth, etc. The modern methods increase dependency on external resources and technical inputs. Preservation of nature in Africa is seriously affected by the so-called new technologies. Multinational corporations in the name of corporate social responsibility bring in such technologies with IPR and other WTO proposals. This trend force people to lose control of their own resources. Exploitation of water deplete resources and the ultimate impact will be on the poor and the marginalised.

The great Mahatma repeatedly appealed that when there are many hands to work and earn their bread, the purpose of mechanisation will serve no purpose for the poor and the marginalised. Livelihood alternatives should have a direct long-term impact on these disadvantaged communities and community mobilisation must presuppose proper awareness for the people so that they make their best choice for their own development.

Some Recommendations

- Outreaching methods need to take stock of different human and material environmental factors and any effort should be RIGHTS BASED.
- Economic empowerment is one of the basic requirements and at the same time, one may consider social and political empowerment of people as well.
- Different communities have their own traditional wealth in terms of their life patterns, practices and resources. Adequate recognition may be given in any strategic plans of outreaching and community mobilisation.

- Community sensitisation in human and child rights issues is an important ingredient in any method so that people may learn to preserve what is their own using external support to refine their own thinking and doing. Technology in external support mission is necessary but very critical in its application. Every community can start with what they have and our outreach methodologies may further enhance what they have and development should start from where they are.
- There are best examples that can set models to these communities to which they should be exposed to achieve the process of self actualisation.
- Multinational corporations and corporates need sensitisation in their social responsibilities and this is possible only for international development organisations if they are really committed to the cause of the poor. Any community outreach package should basically sustain to livelihood alternatives for the people by utilising their own resources and technology transfer need to be handled with very careful considerations.
- Social marketing gains importance but concepts such as BM seeds and other such alternatives should be avoided if we aim at sustainable development. Countries like India take pioneering efforts with strong voluntarism in the field of development but the critical position is to save our communities from development invasion that may do more harm than good.

Conclusion

A very brief analysis is made of the present predicaments of outreaching methods proposed and used by various development organisations. The basic idea may be to sustain the capacity and resourcefulness of people and their environments / contexts in all our methods and strategies of outreaching communities that are disadvantaged.

Chapter 5

Methods of Rural Outreach - Experiments by Gandhigram University

N.Narayanasamy and M.P.Boraian

Gandhigram Rural University (GRU), a premier Rural University in India, is renowned for its rural outreach activities since its origin in 1956. Teaching, Research and Outreach are integral components of the learning process here. Outreach takes place when a change agent works 'for' or 'thro' or 'with' the community, either independently or in association with other change agents – be it a bank, college, corporate, hospital, government or a non-government organisation.

When a university experiments or discovers on its campus, a strategy or a product to solve a critical rural problem (e.g., developing an organic pesticide), it works 'for' the people. When it takes the help of people to disseminate its scientific and technological advancements through contact farmers or conveners of women's groups, or community representatives to reach a larger audience, it works 'through' them. By involving people actively in the process of their developmental transactions, in problem identification, project planning, implementation, monitoring and evaluation stages, outreach agencies work 'with' them. Outreach is also done 'among' people when the agencies stay and work in their target communities.

Proximity with the community in the outreach process decides the extent of involvement of the community - the least in 'for' model to 'less' in 'thro' model, and 'more' in 'with' model to the 'most' in the 'among' model. The 'least' participative models, are 'outreach agency-dominant' whereas the 'most' participative models are 'people-dominant'. The extent of participation of client community in development process depends on the space provided for by the outreach agencies for community participation. The quantum of space provided for by the agencies for people depends on the policies and programmes of the outreach agencies.

Gandhigram gives priority to working 'with and among' people, than 'for and through' people. GRU recognises the primacy of the people in rural development and has always put the people first. People are always consulted; their problems are analysed by themselves in a village gathering; priorities are fixed and solutions are offered by people. This has brought people and faculty members closer. This is a continuous exercise. GRU has experimented with few such methods to work with the people.

University at the Village Doorsteps

'Taking University to the Village Doorsteps' was designed and implemented as an important attempt in making a concerted effort in extension activities. Under this programme, students and teachers drawn from every faculty, department and center selected a village of their choice, and settled down. Individual families, schools, temples, churches, panchayat offices, community centres and health centres served as their abode for a short period though. They worked, learnt, taught, shared, researched, observed, cooked, and rested and relaxed in villages. In the process, they helped to educate, enlighten, empower, counsel, activate and motivate people for improving their knowledge, and awareness, changing their attitude and influencing their behaviour towards better quality of life. Learning from people, however, loomed large in such programmes for the team, although they contributed to their improvement in a small measure.

Activities carried out include undertaking of *shramdan* (manual labour) in the village, organising special camps, demonstration, conducting surveys, arranging visits, dialogue and lectures and organising sports and cultural programmes. *Shramdan* activities ranged from construction of parapet walls, laying of road and playground, planting of seedlings and installation of smokeless *chulha*. Camps comprised a dental camp in a flourosis endemic area and an animal health camp in a farming village. Popularisation of science through awareness, teaching and experiments, computer awareness, chlorination of drinking water, and low-cost supplementary food were the activities taken up for demonstration. Surveys covered themes like status of women, child labour, entrepreneurship, employment and feasibility studies. Interactions took place between students and NGOs, panchayat leaders and government officials. Debating, trekking, meditation and prayers, street plays, cultural programmes and sports competitions were the other activities.

Our students and teachers richly gained from their village stay experience. Their knowledge, skills, attitude, behaviour, and motivation for service registered substantial change in a short period. Every one loved such an experience and longed for similar exposure. Their learning from the village and villagers equipped them with practical knowledge, instilled confidence and made them more resourceful students and teachers. Ultimately, the rural experience enriched the two other components viz., teaching and research. Our teaching and research programmes are therefore, inextricably interwoven with the rural extension programmes.

Gains and Losses

As a result of organising this camp, the distance between students and teachers closed down, understanding between graduate and master's students improved, inter-personal relations between senior and junior Faculty strengthened and the acquaintance between the GRU team and the village cemented. The students managed crisis situations, the faculty tackled complicated issues and together they lubricated the social situations with the villagers wherever there was friction. The teachers involved themselves in *shramdan*, students cooked, and together they learned dignity of labour in practice. The team bore the brunt of local customs in removing shoes while walking through the street or girls being disallowed from temples or the abuses being hurled by persons drunk.

Notwithstanding all these, the students developed 'voluntarism', the sprit of service, helping attitude, ability to withstand difficulties, and managed the crisis wherever possible. People were cooperative by and large, those who were indifferent initially, changed slowly and those who stood at a distance gradually came closer. Our camp belied the traditional theory that it is difficult to enter the village but easy to come out. We learnt that it is easy to enter the village but difficult to come out, because of the bondage and affinity we developed with the community during our stay, work and interaction with the people.

For a few days though, rural communities became our campus, tea stalls served as our libraries, farms and homes became our laboratories, the *shramdan* work sites emerged as our play ground, villagers remained our teachers and their experience sharing turned out to be our textbook. We learnt from the villagers the realities of rural life and were able to comprehend text book theories through this practical exposure. Though this programme was well received by the villagers and acclaimed as a good experiment by the media, it had certain limitations.

Limitations

- In the absence of fully coordinated advance planning of action programmes, many departments ended up conducting their problem-oriented surveys or syllabus-related studies.

- The problems of the villagers were not systematically analysed as a rule. Some villages chosen for the camp were too small to make the villagers visible among the campers.
- Follow-up, being poorer than what was necessary, some of the camps did not contribute to any visible change or development in the villages.

Inspite of these limitations, it could be said that the camps provided a vast scope for the students and staff to understand the rural realities, while staying with the people.

Quadrangular Method

Development will be sustainable, only when there is planning at the grassroot level. Many bottlenecks in development process can be removed, through micro level planning. Realising this, GRU evolved a method called Quadrangular method which involved working with the people. Under this method, in each village, a Planning Committee was constituted with about 10 to 12 apolitical members, giving fair representation to all groups – women, youth, old, socially and economically weaker sections and so on. They were unanimously suggested by the villagers. The elected members of the village planning committee in turn elected among themselves a Chairman, Vice-Chairman and Secretary. The committee thus constituted in each village, met periodically and discussed their problems and priorities.

Based on intensive consultations, a village plan was formulated by the committee. A similar structure was evolved both at the block and district level with respective planning committees. When this exercise was over, a quadrangular meet was arranged wherein government officials, bankers, office-bearers of the planning committees and members of the faculty from Gandhigram Rural University participated. It was a one-day meet. Plans prepared by the Village, Block and District Planning Committee were presented in the meeting. They were examined, refined and finalised. Bank and government officials agreed upon the plans. Representatives of Planning Committee members and faculty members of the university pursued the implementation of the plan.

This method had both strengths and weaknesses. Plans were formulated at the grassroot level. Fair representation was given to all sections of the villages both at planning and implementation stage. Fruits of development were shared by all sections of villages. Government and bank officials were brought closer to villages. People became aware of development programmes undertaken by the government. Sense of involvement was created in the minds of the people.

Limitations

Regarding limitations, the approach tended to deal more readily with superficial issues rather than some fundamental problems which were at the root of backwardness. Planning exercises were carried out by very few representatives of the people. Faculty and students of the university, owing to their academic involvement, could not always find it possible to participate in the planning process with the villagers. Thus, the exercise tended to end up as an endeavour by extension-related people. The government officials always tried to tailor the people's plans to suit the readymade schemes of Government.

Participatory Rural Appraisal

In early 1990s', Participatory Rural Appraisal (PRA) technique was included in the repertoire of people-oriented approaches of the extension programmes at GRU. It involved planning with the people. In the beginning, huge women melas and conferences, consisting of around 1000 women were organised. The purpose was to enable the women to speak out their problems and offer solutions then and there. Rural women conferences were of much help in identifying the problems of women, aspirations priorities, self-confidence and limitations.

Women spoke in such conferences and discussed their issues. Exhibitions were arranged to highlight the problems of women and to demonstrate avenues of income generation activities for women. The basic objective of such conferences was to create an awareness among women and to offer a feeling of empowerment to them. These large melas achieved two things; first the realisation of self-confidence among women; second, the realisation among menfolk that women could talk quite a lot of sense. Yet, problem-solving demanded small groups and more pin-pointed discussions.

Emphasis, therefore, shifted from large melas to specific problems of specific groups such as the youth, aged, landless and so on. The method used in all these meetings was group discussion. In all these, problems were identified by the participants and solutions were arrived at by them. Such day-long sessions were helpful in discussing common problems of the village for quicker appraisal and crisis management.

A series of PRA meetings were held in a number of villages over the years, all of which were day-long deliberations. Based on the receptive nature of participants as well as their positive orientation in working themselves for solving their own problems, GRU started organising workshop which normally took a period of at least two days. The only theme for any PRA meeting in a village is to make the villagers enumerate and analyse their own problems following which they would debate among themselves and would indicate possible solutions.

Strengths and Weaknesses

The villagers felt free and relaxed enough in their interactions. There was the likehood of a more complete debate over any chosen problem because almost all shades and sections of the community were present. The interaction was basically participant (villagers) oriented and not investigator-oriented. It offered much fuller scope for a whole spectrum of reactions – ranging from appreciation at one end and burst of anger at the other. There was room for assuming that any indication of action plan coming out in such meetings would have the tacit approval of the community.

However, such meetings often posed some serious limitations. Few of them were time constraint, and problems which could not be analysed in detail. It led to rushing, imposing ideas and so on. Few individuals tried to dominate; thus, opportunities for all to participate became limited. Further, there was limited scope for participation of a multi-disciplinary team. Formation of group and group discussion was not always easy. Lengthy discussions resulted in brief documentation.

Conclusion

Gandhigram Rural University has been serving as a nursery for innovative outreach activities. Colleges and universities near and far have been transplanting these ideas into their soil and adding their own inputs for their fortification. Curriculum structure of both science and social science programmes have been patterned after the rural realities. Faculty and students share their resources with the neighbouring communities as well as learn from their life and work, in order to understand the practical side of their theoretical exposition in the classroom settings.

Chapter 6

Reaching out to the Rural Communities: An Insight into the Strategies

N.Narayanasamy

Introduction

Change is inherent in nature and human society. The 90s of the last century witnessed tremendous changes. The changes continue. The changes seem to be different in combination of scale, speed, global scope and unpredictability. More seems to be changing and changing faster. Changes are more interconnected and more instantly communicated and yet, the future is harder to predict. The effects of these changes especially on the economic front are more widespread, intensive and dramatic. The advent and practice of the concept of structural adjustments in the form of liberalisation, privatisation, globalisation with growth maximisation strategy have resulted in revolutionary technological innovation, emergence of transnational corporation, new international division of labour, increase in gross national product, and free market economy leading to quality products at reasonable price and so on.

In most countries, however, the combined effects of structural arrangements and desperate investments to promote production for export have had disastrous consequences for the poor. Under free market economy, the state retreats as economy gets globalised; the poorest of the poor are neither able to become full wage earners in the economy nor even full-fledged citizens in the polity. It was found that two-thirds of the world population have incomes that are less than 10 per cent of the per capita income in United States. The data on middle-income countries indicate that the upper 10 per cent clearly participate in capital accumulation and are appropriately rewarded; the lower 40 per cent participate only marginally. The income of the privileged 10 per cent in such countries is 18 times greater than that of the poorest 40 per cent. The situation in the least developed countries is still worse. Thus, the poor are brutally excluded from development.

Alternative Development

But then, to be excluded from development and power is not necessarily to be condemned to a life without history. The excluded poor struggle. They struggle for survival – not alone but with the support of professionals who provide catalytic spark in the face of adversity. Their struggle may take different forms. It might be a peaceful protest movement, it might be individual enterprises in informal economy; it might be emergence of popular economic organisations; it might be self-help movements. Such movements and organisations are considered as the weapons of the weak – weapons to protect themselves from the onslaught of modern capitalism. It is an alternative development strategy which involves a process of social and political empowerment, whose long-term objective is to rebalance the structure of power in society, by making state action more accountable, strengthening the powers of civil society in the management of its own affairs, and making corporate business more socially responsible.

It is centred on people and their environment rather than production and profit. It argues for the rectification of imbalance in social, economic and political power. It is based on humanist model of development - of every man and woman – the whole man and woman – and not just the growth of things, which are merely means. Development is geared to the satisfaction of needs beginning with basic needs of the poor, at the same time development is to ensure the humanisation of man by satisfaction of his need for expression, creativity, conviviality and for deciding his own destiny.

Objectives, Means and Principles

The objective of alternative development is "well-being for all." Well-being is described as the experience of good quality life. It is open to the whole range of human experience, social, mental and spiritual as well as material. It includes living standards, access to basic services, health, good relation with others, friendship, love, peace of mind, choice, creativity, fulfillment and fun and freedom from fear.

The means to achieve the well-being are 'livelihoods security' and 'capability'. Livelihood is defined as the adequate stocks and flows of food and cash to meet basic needs and to support well-being. Security refers to secure rights and reliable access to resources, food and income and basic services. Capabilities refer to what people are capable of doing and being. They help in achieving livelihood security. Capabilities can be enhanced through learning, practice and training. They are the means to better living and well-being.

The principles underlying the objective of well-being are 'equity' and 'sustainability'. Equity includes human rights, intergenerational and gender equity. Sustainability is the core principle of livelihood security and well-being. Sustainability does not imply that there is no change, but that there is an ability to adapt over time. Sustainability has four dimensions: economic, environmental, institutional and social. Economic sustainability is achieved when a given level of expenditure can be maintained over time. Environmental sustainability is attained when the productivity of life supporting natural resources is conserved or enhanced for the use of future generation. Institutional sustainability is ensured when prevailing structures and processes have the capacity to continue to perform their functions over the long run. Social sustainability is realised when social exclusion is minimised and social equity is maximised.

The objectives, means and principles of alternative development are presented in Figure 1.

Figure 1

The Web of Well-being

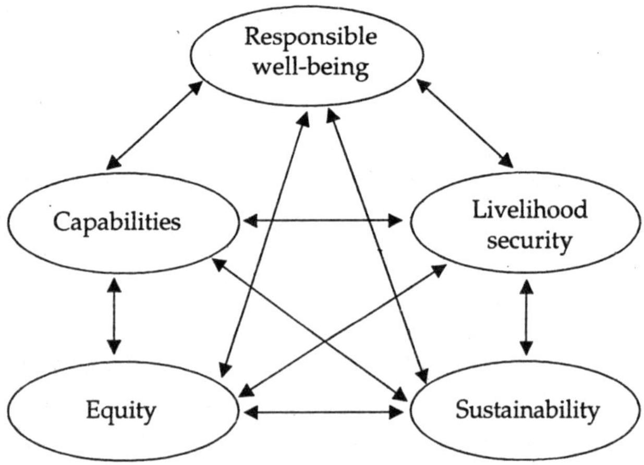

Well-being, capabilities, livelihood, equity and sustainability are inter-connected. The overarching end, in the figure, is well-being, with capabilities and livelihood as the means. Equity and sustainability are principles which qualify livelihood to become livelihood security and well-being to become responsible well-being.

Extension and Alternative Development

The alternative objective of development is "responsible well-being of human beings" or "human development." Extension is development-oriented and development-centred. It strongly believes in the concept of "development with equity" and "sustainable development." Its ultimate aim is to facilitate the creation of self-reliant community. The realisation of this aim requires a much bigger role from the extension personnel. Playing the conventional role of "diffusing or disseminating the information", or "taking the message from "lab to land" or "land to lab" would not in any way help realise the goal of development. They are not mere messengers. The role of a messenger is important. But it is not sufficient. Extension personnel are development facilitators. They are development communicators whose primary role is to "transform the "grassroots" people and enable them to become fully engaged in the process of development and become self-reliant.

In order to effectively perform the role of development communicator, the extension personnel have to constantly monitor the changes occurring in the society, gauge the effects of such changes on human beings and environment, identify the forces and factors responsible for changes, locate the factors which undermine the human development, reposition themselves constantly to face challenges thrown open due to changes and counteract the forces which exclude the "grassroots" people from the process of development. The extension personnel assuming the role of development facilitator/communicator need to be dynamic and proactive. This would require the extension personnel to visit and revisit the strategies that they employ in realising the objective of human development, to discuss and rediscover the strategies, fine-tune such strategies in the context of emerging situation/condition/scenario.

Strategies

A few strategies that would facilitate the extension personnel to perform their tasks more effectively and meaningfully are discussed here. The term 'strategy' denotes the range and combination of activities and choices that development facilitators make or undertake to achieve the development goals. The more choice and flexibility that development facilitators have in their development strategies, the greater their ability to facilitate the process of development. Were is a set of strategies that could be judiciously employed without undermining the principles of equity and sustainability.

Participatory Research

The extension personnel or development facilitator should start with understanding the realities of village life. Alternative development put people at the centre of development. It starts with an analysis of people's livelihood and how it has been changing overtime. It fully involves people and respects their views. How to involve the people in analysing their own conditions? How to ascertain the problems and priorities of the people through the eyes of the people? How to enable the people to look for solutions to the problems? Participatory Research, also known as Action Research, Practitioner Research, Participative Inquiry, Participatory Learning and Action, Participatory Action Research, provides vast opportunity for the people to analyse their own situations and conditions. It aims to enable people who have traditionally been merely the "subjects" of research to take an active part in making their own voices heard. It is a powerful tool, the core process of which is to enable participants to share their perception of a problem, to find common ground and then to engage a variety of people in identifying and testing out some possible solutions. There is a sequence of shared learning for all concerned.

Validation of knowledge and intelligence of the people are central to the participatory research. Research and learning are seen as essentially intertwined. Attention is focused on the processes by which people actually learn, rather than an idea or a factor or a truth or something that exist in abstract. The other key common thread is orientation to action. Participatory research has better chances of leading for solution to problems, because it actively involves those who best understand the issues and have the greatest stake in the issues - community members themselves.

The salient features of participatory research are as follows:

- It basically believes that people are capable of analysing their complex realities. It provides great deal of credence to local people, their knowledge and analytical skills. The role of outsiders is that of a facilitator and convenor. Local people draw, score, rank, analyse and plan.
- The participants - the local people - assume a significant role in deciding the categories and criteria of research.
- It aims at empowering the people. The attempt is to change the existing power relations. The emphasis is to reach out to the most vulnerable, the marginalised, the isolated, the less articulate, the non-literate, women, the aged and children.
- The methods in participatory research use visuals, symbols and flexible local materials like seeds, pebbles, flowers, twigs, soil and powder of different colours. Hence, it is quite conducive to application even with less articulate, shy and illiterate people. It allows them to participate meaningfully in the planning and monitoring of activities.
- It aims at enabling the people to analyse and reflect on their realities so that they can plan for action, implement and monitor their progress. Time and space is also created for the participant to reflect on the process and outputs.
- Participatory research is eclectic. It draws heavily from various disciplines, reports and approaches. It is still evolving. It reinforces the principle of pluralism and diversity because it believes that there are different and innovative ways of doing things.
- The participants from the village own the information. Information gathered is shared among the people and with the outsiders.

Development facilitators have several major advantages in undertaking participatory research. Prominent among them is that the participants 'own' the project and participate in all the activities of the project. It results in sustainability of the development work or activities.

Participatory research requires strong facilitation skills, and interest in research, and interest in solutions. The development facilitators should imbibe the required skills and endeavors to facilitate participatory research among the people.

Methodological Pluralism

India is a land of diversity. There are around 3000 communities and about 360 languages and dialects. These communities vastly differ from each other in terms of language, culture, customs, norms, values, caste, wealth, well-being, livelihood strategies and so on. There is quite a vast and complex diversity even within a community. Hence, it is always difficult to design and adopt a "standardised strategy" to solve the problems. Inspite of that, we have been adopting a standardised strategy as it has its own advantages. First, it minimises administration. Second, it simplifies monitoring, supervision and evaluation. Third, it helps to spend the money fast. But standardisation does not bring the desired results in any development programme as it has failed to take cognisance of diverse and complex nature of the people and their livelihood options and strategies.

Hence, it is essential for the development facilitator to take note, understand, analyse, realise, recognise and value the diversity among the people. Such an understanding and recognition would help them to approach the development process totally from a different angle.

- He would stop repeating the standardised method, approach and strategy
- He would look for new methods and strategies which in turn, would facilitate him to innovate
- He would start practicing pluralistic methodology in development work
- He would develop strong conviction in destandardisation and decentralisation. In short, he would make pluralism central to development.

Think and Link Micro to Macro

Assessing and understanding the ground realities is the first job of a development facilitator. A thorough examination of grassroots situation, using participatory appraisal and analysis would help him to know the status of people, their socio-economic background, the factors which impinge on their lives and livelihoods, their aspirations and priorities and so on. However, the task of the development facilitator does not stop with assessing the condition of the people. It is just a starting point. He has to guide them; assist them by linking them to the external environment and world where there are vast opportunities and potentials and also risks and uncertainties. The development facilitator before guiding the people to the external environment has to be familiar with the external environment. He has to systematically analyze the opportunities available to the people in the external environment, risks and uncertainties in making use of those opportunities.

Such an analysis would not only help him to link the micro realities with macro-perspectives but also enable him to guide the people on the right path. A development facilitator therefore has to think micro, think macro, and link micro to macro. This is all the more important because "happenings" and "changes" at the macro level have a tremendous, immediate and long-term effect on the grassroots people. Hence, a development facilitator has to be very alert, dynamic with a vision and foresightedness to forecast the 'changes' and be ready to face changes and to prepare the people to face uncertainties and challenges.

Build Social Capital

Yet another strategy for effective outreach is building up social capital in the community. Social capital is a social resource. It relates to the formal and informal social relations, which provide vast opportunities for the people to better their living conditions. Social capital is mostly developed through network and connectedness, membership of more formalised groups and relationships of trust, reciprocity and exchanges. Network enhances people's trust and ability to work together which in turn improves their access to wider institutions. Social network facilitates innovations, the development of knowledge and sharing of that knowledge. Membership of formalised groups help in effectively managing the common property resources and the maintenance of shared infrastructure. Relationship of trust, reciprocity and exchanges facilitate cooperation, reduce transaction cost, and provide informal safety net amongst the people especially the poor. Social capital plays a key role in building up human capital.

The development facilitator can and should play key role in facilitating the people especially the poor to build-up social capital. It is a very difficult task, for it is mostly related to cultural and social factors. Factors which promote social capital are: mutual trust, social solidarity, shared interest, willingness to cooperate, willingness to work in a group, faith in team spirit and work and so on. It is not always easy to manipulate. Every community possesses certain amount of social capital; but it varies. Certain communities have high social capital, while certain other communities may have low level of social capital. Levels of social capital are very hard to gauge. They may be discernible only after lengthy analysis.

In building up the social capital, the first step is to assess the extent of social capital present in a community or village.

The second step is to guide them in establishing connectedness with institutions and help them to become members of formal and informal institutions.

The third step is to see who is not having access to social capital; who is excluded from using the benefit arising out of social capital.

The fourth step is to initiate steps to strengthen social capital and help them to make use of the benefits of social capital which include access to information, access to influence or power and to claims or obligations for support from others.

Build, Operate, Turnover CSIs

The development facilitators have to work at different levels - individual, family and community. Sometimes, they may work directly with the people; sometimes, they may work through the groups and institutions especially when common problems and issues crop up in the community. These groups and institutions are called civil society institutions. They are various formations between the level of family and the formal institutions of the state and the market. They include neighbourhood groups, local committees, social clubs, community based organisations and voluntary associations of all kinds.

The public area consists of three institutions *viz* the state, the market and the civil society institutions. They may be compared to vertices of a triangle (See Figure 2).

Figure 2

Institutions

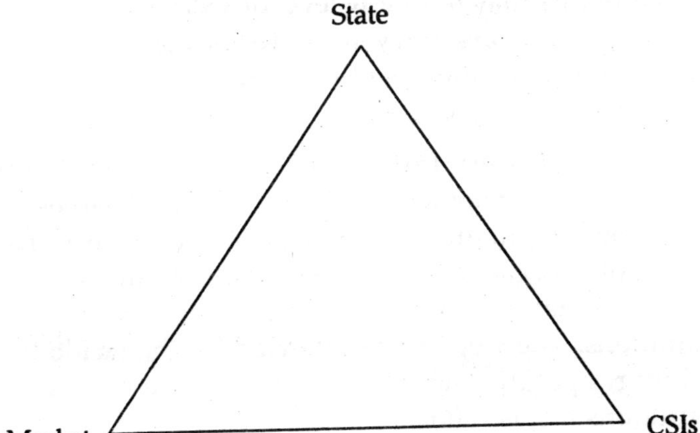

Dominance or overplay of any of these institutions is likely to disturb the equilibrium. The 20th century witnessed a tug-of-war between the state and the market. State institutions dominated during the first half of the last century both in communist and capitalist world. In communist countries, the state controlled the market and the civil society institutions. Even in the capitalist countries, particularly after great depression, Keynes legitimised state control over the economy in the name of 'demand creation' and Roosevelt legitimised the welfare state with New Delhi. Excessive state control especially in communist blocks undermined the freedom of individual, suppression of civil society institutions, restriction of markets and so on.

Market institutions reasserted during the last two decades of the twentieth century with far reaching consequences. Communist states disintegrated. Central planning lost credibility. Public sector has been privatised. The welfare state was dismantled. Reassertion of market forces led to disparity among rich and poor, unemployment, rise of capitalism and so on.

Domination or overplay of either the state or market is likely to disturb the equilibrium. Who would play the role of balancing the activities of the state and market? The civil society institutions have an unenviable position in the system and they would serve as a balancing force between the two. Hence, the need to nurture, develop and strengthen the civil society institutions.

The civil society institutions are the foundations of energy. The development facilitators have to harness this energy for the betterment of the society. They have to ensure that people's organisation at all levels are strengthened and enabled so that they can together act as strong civil society institutions. The steps to be followed by the facilitator in building, operating and handing over the civil society institutions are as follows:

- Identify the existing civil society institutions at the local level through participatory approach
- Study the status of such institutions
- Initiate efforts to strengthen the existing civil society institutions if they are weak
- Facilitate the people to form groups or associations if they are required
- Build the capacity of the people to organise and manage such institutions
- Ensure sustainability of groups or associations promoted

All these efforts would enable the people to have easy access to various forms of capital - physical, natural, social, financial and human. This would also help them to demand the service from the state and to restrict the overplay of market forces.

Establishing Linkages

The linkage process is an important strategy in the integration of poor and depressed sections of the society. Promoting and strengthening civil society institutions largely help the weaker sections to express their voice in the society. The CSIs, to function effectively and to get the people connected to development, need to establish linkage with others. They need to establish linkage among themselves and with others. There are five types of linkages according to Lynton and Pareek. They are: i.) enabling; ii.) functional; iii.) collegial; iv.) normative; and v.) diffusing. Enabling linkages are those which help civil society institutions get started. Functional linkages treated as the warp and weft of the organisation, those which make the organisation to function effectively. It includes field and project staff and infrastructure. Collegial linkages are those that develop among colleagues and professional peers. It would also mean linkages with service providers in government and corporate sectors. Normative linkage stands for certain norms, articulating and practicing those norms, constantly questioning their contemporary relevance and modifying these when needed. Diffusing linkages are a spillover category by which an organisation interacts with the rest of the world.

The development facilitator has to play a very active role in forging various kinds of linkages. Establishing such linkages immensely benefit the people especially the poor in various ways.

First, people get connected to various kinds of welfare and development institutions.

Second, they have easy access to development information and therefore they can make use of the services of development and welfare organisations at less transaction cost.

Third, service becomes demand pull and not supply-push.

Fourth, participation of the people in development initiatives get reinforced.

Fifth, it results in convergence of activities and coordinated efforts of different departments.

The development facilitator, to be effective in playing this role has to perform various tasks which include:

- identification of various institutions in the area,
- assessment of the nature of their works and services provided,
- study of the rules and regulations that govern the provision of services,
- ascertaining the problems and difficulties in providing services,
- examination of strengths and weaknesses in forging linkage among the various institutions; and
- establishing viable linkages wherever possible.

To start with, the development facilitator can think of establishing linkage with various civil society institutions within the village; then he / she can extend the linkage with other state, banking and other organisations.

Putting the First Last

Robert Chambers, in his famous book on *Rural Development: Putting the Last First*, vehemently argued for putting the poor at the centre of development. He said any development process aiming the betterment of poor should see that the physically weak, the isolated, the vulnerable and the powerless are consulted at every stage; their aspirations, priorities and things that matter to them are fully taken into account. The ultimate aim is to empower the people. But then the process of empowerment involves process of disempowerment. In other words, empowerment can take place only when the people who have power and are willing to disempower themselves are prepared to shift themselves from the category of first to the last. This would happen only when there is an attitudinal change among the first and the uppers. Will it be possible? Will the people with power be prepared to disempower themselves? If 'so', how would it happen?

Norman Uphoff has identified a continuum of orientation towards self and others (See Figure 3)

Figure 3

Continuum of orientations towards self and others

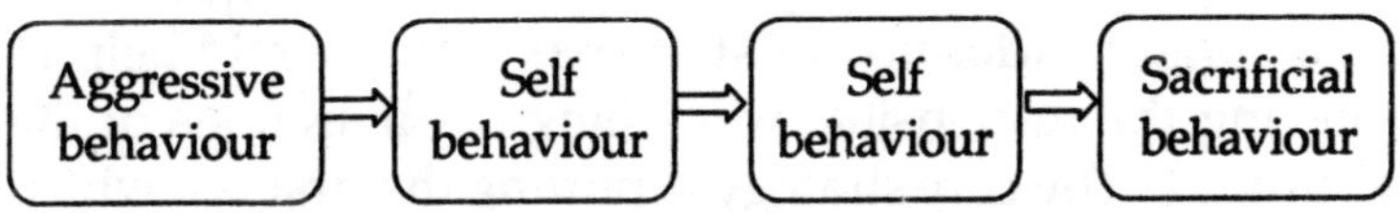

(a) (b) (c) (d)

Aggressive behaviour results in destruction of others. Selfish behaviour is one in which one's gain is another's loss. Generous behaviour is one where everybody gains. It is a win-win situation. Sacrificial behaviour is one which is self destructive in nature. 'Putting the last first' is generous or altruistic behaviour, here, the first remains first, upper remains upper. 'Putting the first last' goes further. It is more radical. It means that those who are powerful disempower themselves and empower others. It implies that the powerful have to give up something.

The process of empowerment may not take place unless the powerful are prepared to disempowers themselves. Since the 'wellbeing' of the poor greatly depends on empowerment, the development facilitator should play a very effective role in empowering and disempowering. First, he / she has to disempower himself / herself. Then he / she may facilitate the process of disempowering the uppers and powerful. This is not an easy task. This requires a great deal of skill. They had to facilitate the gains of disempowerment which include effectiveness, liberation, fulfillment and fun. Disempowerment can liberate uppers from professional prison and personal stress.

Conclusion

Development is both a cause and consequence. There is a two-way relationship between these of change., i.e., development influences and is influenced by change. Change implies physical, technological, economic, social, attitudinal, organisational and political change. A change may be either for good (development), or bad (retrogression). The development facilitator has to see that change facilitates development and ensures equity and sustainability. Adoption of strategies listed would help in achieving the responsible well-being of all sections of the community. The core strategy is putting the first last which require guts and will to change the behaviour of development professionals.

References

1. Department for International Development (2001), **Sustainable livelihood Guidance sheets**, London, October.
2. John Friedman, (1996), **Empowerment : The Politics of Alternative Development**, Blackwell, Oxford, UK.
3. Shirley A.While (1999) (Ed) **The Art of Facilitating Participation,** Sage Publications, New Delhi.
4. Chambers, Robert (1997), **Whose Reality Counts: Putting the First Last**, London.
5. Somesh Kumar (2002), **Methods for Community Participation**, Vistaar Publications, New Delhi.
6. Jan Nerdeveen Peterse, (2001) **Development Theory: Deconstruction / Reconstructions**, Vistaar Publications, New Delhi.
7. Sophie Laws with Caroline Harpear and Rachel Marcus, (2003), **Research for Development**, Vistaar Publications, New Delhi.
8. Chambers, Robert (1983), **Rural Development: Putting the Last First**, London, Harlow.
9. Uphoff Norman, **Learning from Gal Oya : Possibility for participatory Development and Post Newtonian Social Science**, Cornell University Press, Ithaca.
10. Sau Ranjit, (1994) **India : Human Development in a Nation**, Indian Academy of Social Sciences, Allahabad.
11. Singh, Katar, (1986), **Rural Development: Principles, Policies and Management**, Sage Publications, New Delhi.
12. Mikkelsen Britha, (1995), **Methods for Development Work and Research**, Sage Publications, New Delhi.

Chapter 7

Extension in Higher Education in India - The Missing Dimension

G.Palanithurai

People in India and those at the grassroots in particular, are living in a paradoxical situation. Opportunities for amassing wealth by a few and possibilities of marginalising or excluding people from the process of development are greater as the new economic movement of liberalisation, privatisation and globalisation, is fast catching up. Those who understand the process easily exploit the opportunities and amass wealth whereas those who do not understand the process and lack the capacity are totally marginalised and excluded from the process of development. The developed societies, with their economic advancement, speedy technological development, perfect handling of the technology and enhanced capacity have outwitted the developing societies in terms of development. The gap between the technology and the capacity of the people to handle technology is wider in developing societies.

The communities in the rural areas and the slums in the urban areas are facing scores of problems. Most of the problems are related to lack of awareness and poor skills among the people. Many of the problems of the communities and especially the poor can be solved very easily if the educational institutions are involved in community service through systematic extension activities. Medical colleges, through their extension activities, could treat poor patients at their place through their transportation. Agricultural colleges can disseminate technical knowhow to the farming communities through their scientists. Arts and science colleges can create awareness among the people regarding their livelihood. Technical institutions can develop appropriate technologies and hand them over to the rural people. Moreover, they can equip the people with greater skills with self-employment potentials. Total literacy can be achieved with the active participation of higher education institutions. In many of the southern states, this could be achieved within a short span of time. Awareness on the decent living conditions of the human beings can be created among the people.

Even after 54 years of democratic governance and implementation of series of rural development schemes for the poor, still people live in sub-human living conditions. On the contrary, the number of educational institutions are on the rise. Engineering colleges, medical colleges, para professional colleges, private universities and other higher educational institutions have been constantly growing. At present, many of the institutions have been started in the rural areas as they get adequate water free of cost and space. When more and more educational institutions are in the process of producing graduates, the society gets more literate and qualified personnel for service. But why then the problems of the poor are also growing and becoming so critical? There are a number of factors responsible for the conditions of the poor in the society, of which, the non-existence of the linkage between the society and the educational institutions is one of the prime factors.

All the higher educational institutions have several extendable aspects, namely information, knowledge, skills, technology, service and so on. But the institutional structure is not oriented to extend the best to the society. Further, the institutions do not have the mechanism to convert the available extendables in a form suitable to the requirements of the community. Many believe that the Agriculture

Faculty alone can do extension work. Every department and discipline can do extension work provided they know the strategy and the method. Even in the UGC framework, extension is assigned only to the Adult and Continuing Education Department. Unfortunately, in many State Universities, this department has been closed.

Thus extension, the third and vital dimension of higher education, is neglected now. The gap between the higher education institutions and the society therefore, has to be bridged. The extendables available in the higher education institutions have to be extended to the society for the benefit of both through a system of Extension Education and Extension Service. In order to perform the above tasks, the disciplines in the higher education have to be reclassified. Higher educational institutions can be grouped according to their nature and character. Some of the institutions can create awareness among the people. Many of the institutions and departments can deliver services directly to the people. A few institutions and departments can transfer skills and build the capacity of the rustic folk who perform difficult roles and tasks.

Classification of Clusters

Cluster	Discipline	Methodology
Cluster I	Maths Chemistry Physics Zoology Botany Computer	Indirect and Intermittent Societal contact
Cluster II →	Economics Public Administration Political Science Business Management Sociology Psychology Languages Home Science Legal Studies →	Direct Continuous Systemic Syllabus oriented Societal contact
Cluster III →	Medicine Sanitation Agriculture Technology Engineering Pharmacy Paramedical →	Direct Continuous Systemic Service oriented Technology oriented Skill oriented Cognition oriented Societal contact

I	Continuously working with a target group	Institutions and departments continuously working with the target group, namely, ultra-poor, women, dalits, children, disabled, artisans and farmers
II	Continuously working on an issue	Institutions and departments can work on issues, namely, sanitation, water supply, poverty reduction, agriculture, skills upgradation, education, etc.
III	Delivering services on wheels	Institutions and departments can place the extension materials in their vehicles, visit communities and offer their services and at their doorsteps
IV	Dissemination of information	Institutions and departments can provide useful, processed and packaged information to the different stakeholders in society
V	Building the skills and capacity	Institutions and departments can build the skills and capacity of stakeholders and service providers and user groups
VI	Skills upgradation	Institutions and departments can reinvent old skills, reinvigorate skills and upgrade the skills which are in vogue to the level of the market conditions
VII	Assisting the delivery system	Institutions and departments can provide assistance to service providers, in the form of technology, skills and capacity
VIII	Assisting development organizations	Institutions and departments can assist the development organizations and institutions which are working in the rural areas by building their skills and capacity
IX	Establishing forward and backward linkages	Institutions and departments can create and promote linkages among the institutions and organizations working for the poor

Gist: Information, Awareness, Skill, Capacity, Technology and Service

Sl. No.	Activities	Institutions/Departments
1.	Farm Input Farm Activities Farm Practices Farm Technology	Agriculture Faculty
2.	Animal Husbandry	Veterinary Faculty/College/ University
3.	Water supply and Sanitation Water recycling Waste disposal	Civil Department in Engineering College Sanitation Department in Medical College Medical College Chemistry Department in Arts and Science College
4.	Ante-natal care Natal-care Post-natal care	Medical College Home Science Department Centre for Women Studies
5.	Child Care	Medical College Home Science Department
6.	Youth Development	Department of Youth Affairs/ Development
7.	Panchayat Management Governance	Public Administration Political Science
8.	Adult Literacy	Adult and Continuing Education, Language Departments
9.	Rights of Women, Children and Dalits	Legal Studies
10.	Women Empowerment SHG activities Management Gender equality	Women Studies Centres Home Science Department Sociology Department
11.	Natural Resources Management	Environmental Studies Centres Botany Department

12.	Public Distribution System Poverty surveys Poverty reduction strategies	Economics Department
13.	Use of solar energy Energy Management Energy Technology	Physics Department Energy Department
14.	Peoples' skills and technology for Economic Activities	Rural Industries and Management Department
15.	Herbal alternative medicine Nature cure	Pharmacy Department Botany Department Zoology Department
16.	Best practices in the community for livelihood Tribal studies and welfare Conflict resolution	Sociology Department Anthropology Department Gandhian Studies/Peace Studies Department
17.	Imbibing cooperative spirit and inculcating repayment ethics among borrowers	Cooperation Department
18.	Taking information, communication, technology (ICT) to rural areas	Computer Centres
19.	Micro level planning Resource surveys	Rural Development Department Geography Department
20.	Population awareness Family welfare promotion	Demography Department
21.	Prevention and promotion of Culture and Art Awareness about national leaders, freedom fighters	History Department

The above list is only an illustrative but not exhaustive.

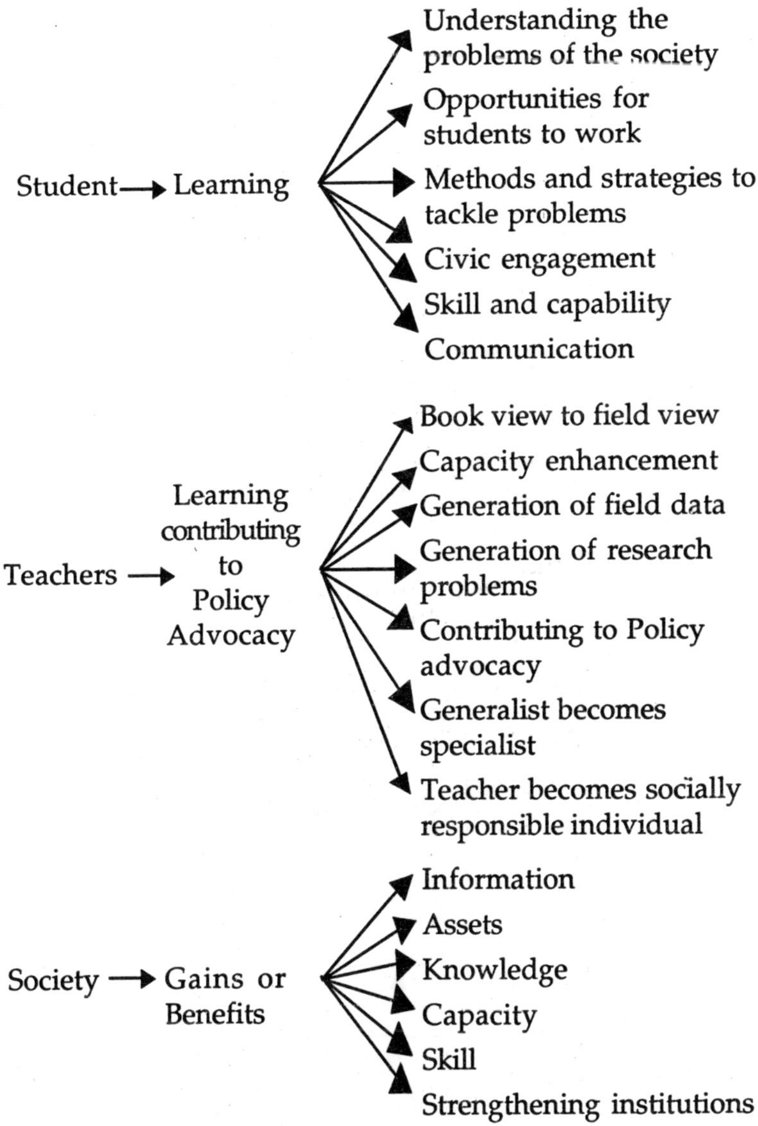
Student → Learning
Understanding the problems of the society
Opportunities for students to work
Methods and strategies to tackle problems
Civic engagement
Skill and capability
Communication
Teachers → Learning contributing to Policy Advocacy
Book view to field view
Capacity enhancement
Generation of field data
Generation of research problems
Contributing to Policy advocacy
Generalist becomes specialist
Teacher becomes socially responsible individual
Society → Gains or Benefits
Information
Assets
Knowledge
Capacity
Skill
Strengthening institutions

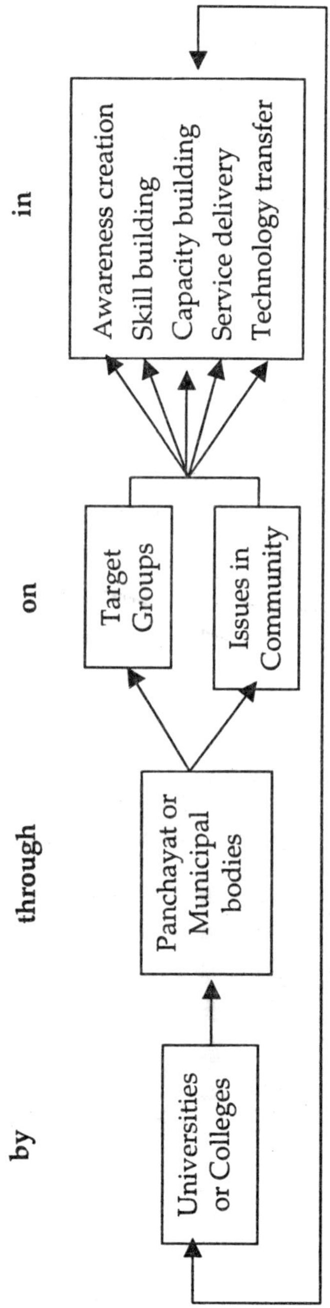
by
through
on
in
Universities or Colleges
Panchayat or Municipal bodies
Target Groups
Issues in Community
Awareness creation
Skill building
Capacity building
Service delivery
Technology transfer

Higher Educational Institutions should have a linkage with the grassroots institutions both in the rural and urban areas for their extension activities on a sustainable basis. Every institution should have a clear cut approach for its extension activities. While carrying out extension activities, the higher educational institutions can either work in a social group or in a geographical area on issues facing the community. Their activities may encompass creating awareness, building skills and capacity, delivering services, evolving technologies and transferring these technologies.

Gandhigram Model

The above framework of Extension was developed from the experience of Gandhigram Rural University. In Gandhigram, extension is an integral component of the whole education system and process.

It has the following objectives:

- to enrich the learning process of students and faculty through exposure to community needs, problems and issues;
- to impart training in development-oriented activities to grassroot development workers, officials and non-officials drawn from NGOs, government departments, banks, training and research organisations;
- to organise knowledge and skill-based training for a wide spectrum of clients from local institutions such as Panchayats, cooperatives and other community-based formal and informal organisations;
- to undertake socially relevant action-oriented research and analysis for the betterment of the rural community; and
- to bring out changes in the living conditions of different sections of the rural community.

Methods

The above objectives are being realised through a series of activities by adopting the following methods:

1. Women Melas (of SHGs)
2. Field visits
3. Camps
4. Awareness camps
5. Training programmes
6. Rallies and processions
7. Skill building workshops
8. Capacity building workshops

Illustrative list of Activities done by the Departments at Gandhigram Rural University

1. Department of Political Science: Building the capacity of Local Body leaders and helping the Gram Panchayats to prepare perspective plan
2. Department of Rural Industries and Management: Training village youth and SHG women in skills to develop micro enterprises and village industries
3. Department of Extension Education: Monitoring and evaluation of projects, training the NGO representatives in management of rural projects, preparation of rural development projects for NGOs, donor agencies and government.
4. Department of Agriculture and Animal Husbandry: Train farmers increase productivity and to sustain profit—to train SHG women in dairying
5. Department of Sanitation: Developing low cost sanitary material and conducting training to local body leaders and engineers of Government Departments

6. Department of Sociology: Creating awareness among the marginalised about their rights and opportunities for development
7. Department of Cooperation: Training the functionaries in cooperatives, creating awareness on repayment ethics
8. Rural Technology Centre: Developing cost effective technology and propagating in village communities
9. Department of Home Science: Creating awareness among the women about their results and opportunities
10. Department of Biology: Training the SHG women in Horticulture, Vermiculture, Sericulture and Bio-technology
11. Department of Physics: Installing smokeless chulas and training village women in using the same
12. Department of Chemistry: Creating awareness among the people about environment and helping the local community to get safe drinking water supply
13. Department of Mathematics: Training school teachers in villages in Mathematics and teaching about latest development
14. Department of Computer Science: Training the rural youth and SHG women in computer operations
15. Department of Economics: Identification of vulnerable families
16. Department of Rural Development: Helping the Panchayats in micro level plan and women empowerment
17. Department of Applied Research: Taking up social problems for action research
18. Department of Gandhian Thought & Peace Science: Taking Gandhiji's ideals to villages and working for conflict resolution

Resource Mobilisation

Enormous amount of resources are available at every level for public service. In the era of globalisation, resource mobilisation is not a difficult task. The Government provides enormous amount of money for IEC activities that can be tapped. All companies have to spend a portion of their profit for social service as a mandate and they are ready to provide resources. The banking sector has a specific allocation for such service activities to the society. There are non-government organisations and voluntary organisations which can be used for this purpose. There are a lot of funding agencies in the country to support extension activities which can be tapped efficiently. Lions Clubs and Rotary Clubs can also be used. For many of the activities, people themselves will contribute. At the university level and the college level, what is needed is commitment and a sense of dedication and a set of effective strategies. Gandhigram has been supported by a slew of donors both governmental and non-governmental in the promotion of scores of activities listed above (Their list is annexed for the benefit of those interested in contacting them for their proposed activities).

Outcome of this Extension

Extension services in rural communities will generate an array of benefits to the people in difficulties. Villages will get clean drinking water supply. Hundred per cent literacy will be achieved. All eligible children will be enrolled in schools. There won't be any malnourished child in the rural areas and any anaemic patient among pregnant women. IMR will be reduced and babies will be born in the rural areas with correct weight. Shelter can be provided to all. PDS shops will provide the entitlements to the poor. The skills of the people will be used profitably. They will gain access to the market provided with the needed technology for their secure livelihood and they will start living in humane conditions.

People will have development aspirations and they will be conscious of development. The marginalised, poor, women and dalits will be empowered. People will have necessary awareness on their rights and duties. Students and teachers will know the social reality in all its aspects and they will be conscious of social service. A responsible good society and good governance can be established by ensuring the university systems be more responsive to the needs and problems of the community and the interests and demands of the society.

Conclusion

Thus every college and every university has to first assess what they can extend to the society and identify the extentables namely, ideas, knowledge, information, skill, capacity, technology and strategy. Further, the institutions have to evolve appropriate methodological designs to do extension activities. It is further necessary to identify the partner institutions and organisations to carry out the extension activities by providing necessary resources and wherewithals. Finally, the extension activities have to be integrated with the curriculum for its sustainability so that most of the ills facing the society could be easily cured.

Chapter 8

Community Outreach Methodologies of a Women's University

Thangamani Swaminathan

Development of the Country in the true sense means development of the rural communities. Apart from the efforts of the government, all sections of the community are responsible for reaching out to the people with suitable programmes. The Non-Governmental Organisations, educational institutions, service organisations and institutions and individual philanthropists also take initiatives in bringing about positive changes in the communities.

The educational institutions, especially universities have a vital role to play, through their teaching, research and outreach activities. The curriculum of Higher Education including outreach methodologies helps in moulding the citizens towards community service. The students should realise that they are indebted to the community, from which they are hailing from. The resources for education are the inputs from the community. This awakening is to be reiterated in the minds of students, at all levels of education. In the following pages, the community outreach methodologies followed by Sri Avinashilingam Education Institutions, with its Pre-School, Elementary School, Higher Secondary School and University level programmes, are reviewed.

Outreach through Pre-Schools

The teachers and assistants of the child care institutions/support services are being trained to develop skills and abilities to plan appropriate and challenging programmes through play way approaches. They have also been equipped to maintain community contacts; involve parents and the larger community in organising and monitoring pre-school programmes and thereby elicit community participation effectively.

Tasks Accomplished

- service of parent education classes on important issues such as breast feeding, immunisation, ORT, health check up, balanced diet including low-cost nutritious recipes, needs and rights of children, training children in desirable hobbies, small family norm, low cost play equipment and household technology, etc. The feed back from parents showed that these parent education classes have enriched parents, especially mothers in terms of knowledge and skills
- Mothers are trained to prepare low-cost play equipments and offer them to Anganwadi children.
- The community members join to create conducive physical set up for the Anganwadis
- The members in the community are involved in the conduct of pre school programme such as celebrating functions, field trips and story narrations
- Women's groups are formed to mobilise resources for the creative use of their children in the pre-schools
- Doctors, police men/ police women, post-man/post woman, craft workers and other community workers and small-scale industrialists in the parent community offer their might to promote perception of the growing children, explaining their role in the community
- Exhibition and mass meetings arranged by the community in collaboration with the preschools/ crèches sensitise the community on important issues related to parenting and educating children, in addition to ways and means of better living

- The pre-schools/ crèches monitored by Sri Avinashilingam Institutions have also led us towards consoling parents, children with challenging needs and deviant children
- Volunteers in the community have been trained to identify the disabled and refer them to our institutions and integrated education
- Community based rehabilitation for the disabled was tried to train the disabled in self- help skills

Outreach through Primary School

The Primary School is used as a vehicle to take the messages to the families and thereby to the community. The children are given nutrition education, health education and personal hygiene; they in turn, take the knowledge to their family members.

The children conduct literacy classes to their neighbours. As members of the Red Cross, children are trained in first aid. The Parent Teacher Association is very active conducting education programmes for mothers on handicrafts, nutrition, child care and they also participate in the uplift of the school. All India Radio is utilised by the school, to disseminate the information needed for the total development of the children. Integrated education for the visually handicapped children is part of the primary school programme. It is really a community service carried out by the teachers of the school.

Outreach through Higher Secondary School

Apart from the class room teaching, students are given exposure to the activities, namely, National Cadet Corps, National Service Scheme, Girl Guides and Junior Red Cross. The students are trained in community outreach even in their curriculum through vocational courses

In the School programme, on every Wednesday, two periods are allotted for the activities related to outreach programmes. Trained teachers impart special training to the students. To enrich the experience of the students, they are taken for community work in the field. The celebration of National Days elicits the participation of the school in the community work.

Outreach Methodologies at the University Level

As the University is part of the society, the curriculum is framed, based on the social needs. Accordingly, the outreach methodologies are also to be selected, suitable for the changing requirements of the community. Hence, no curriculum or methodology can remain static.

The National Service Scheme at the Under Graduate level and Community and Social Service Programme at the Post Graduate level are curricular components. The National Cadet Corps, Rotary Club, Red Ribbon Club, Planning Forum and SHGs through Women Development Corporation are other means of reaching the community by the students. The Computer Literacy programme by the Centre for Women's Studies and activities of the Gandhian Studies Centre on and off the campus, provide opportunities to the students for serving the community.

The research programmes of the Post Graduate Students, especially from the Home Science Faculty, are community oriented and the students conduct field experiments. Apart from that, the research departments have linkages with national and international organisations, their experiments are conducted in the communities. Even the industrial linkages of the University aim at the uplift of the communities.

Typology of Approaches

The methodologies followed in the outreach efforts include individual, group and mass approaches, suitable for the subject matter.

Individual Approach

Personal contact is considered as an effective means of reaching out to the illiterate masses in the community. In conducting a bench mark survey and developing rapport with the communities, the students visit individual households. Individual approach becomes important in organising certain education programmes on small family norm, and HIV/AIDS awareness.

Group Approach

The students camp in the villages aim at learning about village life and educating people on the various aspects of better family living. *Shramdan* is practiced in the communities, to create physical assets and establish infrastructure in the Anganwadies and schools; organising camps is considered to be very important to elicit people's participation and voluntary action. The camp life gives hands on experience to the students about the village life, existence of poverty and other problems in the community, culture and values of their community, availability of infrastructure and resources, programmes and schemes of the government in operation, grassroots level extension workers and their performance and community organisations and institutions. The camp experience is a platform for students to learn about the reality and inspires them to decide and work for the community development.

At the same time, certain activities of the students require camping in the village. The PG students of Home Science Faculty camp in the villages to study the nutritional status and educate the people on rich nutrition. Nutrition education includes the use of all the outreach approaches and extension teaching methods.

The University conducts seminars and workshops to transfer the message to community – school teachers, anganwadi workers, elected members of local governments, SHG members and the local leaders. Summer camps are organised for school children on values, skills and knowledge making them as good citizens.

Mass Approach

Campaigns and public meetings are organised in rural and urban communities to create awareness. The themes for such mass approaches were education on health and hygiene to protect people from communicable diseases, awareness on HIV/AIDS, small savings and voter awareness. The news paper is used as an important mass media to communicate to the people on different programmes and activities of the university. Folk media is used for suitable themes to reach people.

Linkages with Institutions

Jan Shiksha Sansthan

The University is doing commendable service to the community by training educated unemployed youth in house wiring, motor winding, vehicle repairing, refrigeration and air conditioning and computer service through JSS sponsored by Ministry of Human Resource Development.

Krishi Vigyan Kendra

The Avinashilingam Krishi Vigyan Kendra provides training to practicing farmers and farming women in improved agriculture, post-harvest technology, health, nutrition, environmental hygiene, low cost technology, water management, water recycling and better family living.

Publications

News Letter

The University is publishing the News Letter of the university every semester to acquaint the academic world with the educational programmes undertaken by the students and teachers of the various faculties.

Indian Journal of Nutrition and Dietetics

The University is publishing a widely circulated quarterly Journal - the Indian Journal of Nutrition and Dietetics which carries standard scientific articles related to the fields of Foods, Nutrition and Dietetics. The Institute had initiated this Journal in the year 1964. The findings of several research studies undertaken by the Institute have been reported at National and International meetings, journals and in other publications.

Vignana Chudar

Vignana Chudar is a popular scientific monthly magazine started in the year 1974 and is being published in Tamil for the benefit of students, home makers and the community. The latest findings of Science and Technology are given in simple language in a precise manner.

Research Highlights

Research Highlights is a quarterly published from the university in January, April, July and October. It publishes current research papers and review articles in the fields of Home Science, Science, Humanities, Education and Social Sciences. The journal is of tremendous significance to the students and faculty of Home Science, Science, Agriculture, Humanities, Education, Social Sciences and allied fields.

Other Publications

Nearly 50 pamphlets and brochures have also been published in order to cater to the needs of students, researchers, development professionals, social workers and functionaries at the field level.

Conclusion

Avinashilingam University for Women is firmly committed to the education of skilled workers for the world of work, with deep resolve to serve the community. But for the services of this university, women in many families in

Coimbatore would have stopped their education at the higher secondary level and confined themselves to their domestic spheres. Unlike the traditional universities which emphasise routine conventional disciplines, Avinashilingam University has shown that the application of modern science and technology to family and community living practices, would improve dramatically the quality of life in terms of health, well being and productivity. The services of the university are sought as a consultancy agency by the Departments of Social Welfare, Industries, Agriculture, Education, Rural Development and Health of the Central and State Governments and international organisations. The University will continue to strive to be socially relevant in whatever programme it takes up in terms of teaching, research and outreach, with suitable methodologies.

Chapter 9

Community Outreach Programmes at Gandhigram - An Overview

M.P.Boraian

Gandhigram is as old as the independent India, for it was established during 1947, by the dedicated disciples of Mahatma Gandhi Dr.G.Ramachandran and Dr. Soundram Ramachandran. When India became independent, Gandhiji urged all his disciples to span out to various parts of the country and spread his ideals by serving the poor and distressed. Gandhigram was thus a deliberate choice, born to serve as a social service laboratory. With a team of social workers, this couple struggled to eradicate poverty and eliminate ignorance from the villages around through various activities like crèche, clinic, and cottage industries.

Nearly 10 years later, was born Gandhigram Rural Institute, as a culmination of various activities under education from crèche to a college, initiated during this period. Established under the auspices of National Council for Rural Higher Education (Ministry of Education, Govt. of India), GRI was one of the 14 Rural Institutes which functioned in various parts of the country. In the course of their functioning, while all the other 13 Rural Institutes got affiliated to their neighbouring universities, GRI stood alone and pursued its mission of taking higher education to the rural youth.

By the end of nearly 20 years, GRI was conferred the status of Deemed University by the University Grants Commission (UGC), Government of India. Ever since GRI became a Deemed University, the Faculties, departments, courses and community service activities grew steadily and the number of teachers and students rose constantly. Almost after a quarter century of service as a Deemed University, Gandhigram Rural Institute was accorded five star status by the National Assessment and Accreditation Council (NAAC), set up by the University Grants Commission. GRI has now become Gandhigram Rural University (GRU).

Extension is Central

Community Development and Extension was established as one of the first departments in GRU as early as 1956 when the institute was born. Extension programme carried out by GRU in its rural hinterlands for nearly half a decade was one of the primary factors which influenced the decision of NAAC. Prescribing a uniform policy of higher education for the country, UGC advocated the system of teaching, research and extension for adoption by all the colleges and universities in 1976, 20 years after Gandhigram Rural Institute had embarked upon rural extension activities in the service of the community. It was, therefore, a fitting recognition that the UGC invited Gandhigram Rural Institute to serve as a member of the committee constituted by UGC, in the process of evolving this tri-focal teaching, research and extension policy.

Though extension was placed third by UGC, GRU accords a pivotal place for extension. Extension component thus remains central and is inextricably interwoven around both teaching and research. Consequently, all the three components are integrally linked with one another. Unlike in other colleges and universities, rural extension programmes in the service of the hinterland communities command a prime place in the policies and programmes of GRU. Extension is therefore not merely a third dimension as in other colleges and universities, but is accorded an equal, and central place in the hierarchy of GRI's activities.

Objectives

GRU stands for Gandhian ideas of education with the following objectives:

1. To provide for instruction and training in branches of learning as will promote a classless and casteless society,
2. To undertake research and help in the advancement and dissemination of knowledge; and
3. To function as a centre for extension work leading to integrated rural development.

Under instruction and training, GRU offers courses with a definite rural bias. All the research activities have 'people' and 'issues' as the focus. Extension activities revolve around backward rural communities with emphasis on the rural poor, *dalits*, the aged and women and children.

Typology of Activities

This work makes an attempt to portray the outreach programmes of GRU, with a view to highlight the various dimensions and dilemmas involved in the process.

GRI undertakes three types of outreach activities viz.

- o Institute–based
- o Department–based and
- o Student–based

Under 'Institute–based' activities, the following activities are undertaken:

Institute sponsored

Institute centred activities include Balwadi in 13 service villages with the support of Central and State Social Welfare Boards since 1975, social infrastructure based activities such as housing for the *dalits* in 30 villages with the support of a German funding agency, and community organisation based activities such as *Mahalir Mandrams* (now SHGs), Youth clubs, Village Planning Commission, Balar sabhas, Peace brigades, and Science clubs. Programme or Service based activities such as total rural transformation project in a *dalit* village with CAPART funding or a community bio-gas project in a backward village with Department of Science and Technology funding formed another dimension. Almost all the activities sponsored by the institute are coordinated the Department of Extension.

Department initiated

Department-based activities is relatively a recent phenomenon, especially after every department tapped various external sources of funding for the department specific projects. Department of Science and Technology funding for drinking water project by Home Science, Department of Bio-Technology funding for mushroom cultivation by Biology, and Tamil Nadu Energy Development Authority funding for smokeless chulah project by Physics Department are some of the examples.

Student centred

Outreach activities by students are as old as the institute. Even before moving into the villages, students and teachers built up the campus brick by brick, particularly through common amenities such as road formation, play ground preparation, farm operations, maintenance of hostel premises and reaching out to the neighbouring villages.

Village camps forms an essential component of every course and formed part of their course requirement. Every camp is organised for a duration of seven days as at present. Every camp involves certain major components such as community life, learning about rural realities from the people, study of rural problems, organising cultural programmes with development messages and formation of community-based organisations.

Weekly extension programmes ranging from half-a-day to whole day give the students and teachers an opportunity to make curriculum-based study of rural life through meetings, discussions, surveys or participatory rural appraisal methods. Besides interaction with the people, students also visit institutions such as village panchayats, cooperative societies, schools, health centres, or people's organisations such as SHGs, Youth clubs, etc. Select students who join NSS also take part in short duration camps and undertake community service activities.

Besides village visits, students also visit public institutions such as Non-Government Organisations, Government departments (Block Development Offices, District Rural Development Agencies and District level Development Departments), Industrial houses, financial institutions (Banks, Cooperatives) and other public centres such as Farmers Market *(Uzhavar Santhai)*, Cattle Shandy for practical learning and study tours to premier Rural Development related institutions which widen the horizon of students' knowledge.

Technology Training

Faculties and Departments provide training for the rural youth, adolescent girls and SHG members through short duration trainings in the following spheres:

- Spirulina cultivation
- Sericulture cultivation
- Vermin composting
- Mushroom cultivation
- Smokeless *chulah*
- Hand pump repair
- Electrical wiring
- Masonry work

Rural youths are also trained in industries and trades such as bakery products, value addition in handlooms, soap production, paper conversion, natural dyes, garments production, fruit preservation, cost effective housing and related technologies.

Surveys and Studies

Under the guidance of expert faculty, students and scholars along with the field staff, undertake surveys and studies on multitude of themes. Surveys on literacy, health, nutrition, energy, resource endowment, industrial potentials, and livestock position, besides bench mark and socio-economic surveys are some of the prominent ones. Studies on awareness of villagers about Govt. programmes, HIV/AIDS, social issues such as female infanticide, child labour, and street children, hunger, micro nutrient deficiency, rural indebtedness, landless agricultural workers, tribals and plantation workers are worth mentioning.

Awareness Programmes

GRI organises series of awareness programmes on the following themes through cultural programmes:

- Organic farming
- Watershed development
- Environment
- Public Health and Sanitation
- Evils of alcoholism
- Life of Gandhiji
- Computer awareness
- HIV/AIDS
- Functional literacy
- Legal protection for women
- Voter awareness
- Consumer awareness

Health Camps

In active collaboration with specialist hospitals, GRU organises a series of camps in villages in the vicinity of Gandhigram. Eye camp (by Arvind Eye Hospital, Madurai), Veterinary camp (by Tamil Nadu University of Veterinary Sciences), and General Medical Check-up camp (by Meenakshi Mission Hospital, Madurai) are some of the prominent camps.

Leadership and Skill Training

Political Science department trains village panchayat leaders, cooperation department trains leaders of cooperatives and commercial crop production farmers, Rural Industries department trains entrepreneurs, Rural Technology centre trains rural artisans, Rural Development department trains SHG women, Adult Education and

Extension Department trains village extension workers and Agriculture Faculty trains progressive farmers.

Centre for Entrepreneurship Development, Rural Technology Centre and Krishi Vigyan Kendra train rural youth, adolescent girls, SHG members and farm women in multiplicity of vocational and income generating skills leading to enrichment of their existing economic activities and setting up self employment ventures with their own or externally mobilised resources.

People's Organisations

GRU has been instrumental in motivating people for organising local organisations with people's involvement. Self Help Groups (SHGs), Youth Clubs, Village Planning Committees, Peace Committees, Balar Sabhas and Science Clubs, Farmers Associations, and Rural Radio Forums have been organised by various faculties and departments. Recently, the dept. of Cooperation has organised coconut growing farmers into Coconut Farmers Marketing Associations in 12 villages, and Consumer Clubs in 43 Schools under the auspices of NSS. Department of Adult Continuing Education and Extension has organised 63 women and 15 men Self Help Groups in five block (i.e. Athoor, Batlagundu, Nilakottai, Dindigul and Reddiarchatram) with about 1000 members from 63 villages, with the saving of Rs. 4.5 lakhs per year. It has also organised Population clubs in Colleges and Universities in Tamil Nadu. While GRU Library has established 12 Rural Libraries, Physical Education Department. has organised 10 Rural Sports Clubs in villages.

Teaching Rural Children

Providing supplementary teaching support to children in rural schools as well as training teachers in these village schools in certain subjects, conventionally considered as tough, constitutes an essential component of GRU's extension activities in the realm of rural education. Science

English, Mathematics, Physics, Chemistry and Biology subjects are taught by the respective Faculties/ Departments to school children at various levels ranging from I std to XII, during class hours, in the evenings, during week ends and in the summer. Teachers in these schools are also trained by GRU in coaching their students on tough subjects, using simple methods.

Besides the rural schools in our service villages, this programme also benefits the inmates of an orphanage (Children's home), a special school for widows, destitutes and the separated women, (Kasturba Sevikashram) and a service oriented (Kasturba) Hospital run by Gandhigram complex of institutions. In one instance, a Chemistry teacher on leave for 6 months from a service village school was ably substituted by the Chemistry Department of GRU, through Post graduate students who taught the school students, by rotation.

Supply of Science Kits to 10 Schools, demonstration with scientific equipments in rural schools and display of computer and its operations by the various science departments also deserve mention. Towards taking information and communication technology to the rural children, the role of Computer Science Department stands out. Training provided by this department in desktop operation (DTP) for the rural youth, and internet, digital photography, Offset printing and word processing for the SHG women will enable the village people to benefit by the information technology.

Besides Science teaching, value education forms another vital element of our rural education programme. School students are imparted value education by GRU students and staff from Department of Adult Education and Extension Education, ably supported by English and Science Faculties. Value education constitutes the core of our extension programmes, aimed at creating young human resource with values and dedication to the community and the nation.

Resource Support

In addition to its internal resources, GRU draws infrastructural and resource support from varied institutions and organisations committed to the cause of our rural brethren. Regular programmes and centres such as National Service Scheme (NSS), Krishi Vigyan Kendras (KVK), Information Development and Resource Agency (IDARA), Energy centre and special projects such as Diabetes Prevention and Research with Home Science Department, Mushroom Technology project with Biology Department, Information village project with Computer Science Department, Counselling Services with Adult Education Department, Human Resource Development Centre with Faculty of Rural Health and Sanitation, Watershed/Organic farming technology with Faculty of Agriculture constantly feed into the fabric of our rural extension programmes.

Foreign donor agencies including bilateral agencies and United Nations Organisations such as World Health Organisation (WHO), UNFPA, World Bank, Ford Foundation, Central and State Government departments of various ministries through their various welfare and development programmes, reputed research and development bodies like ICAR, ICSSR, ICMR, KVIC at the national level, Specialist Institutions and Research Centres such as M.S. Swaminathan Research Foundation, also lend their share in the process of our extension programmes.

Strategies and Methods

GRU adopts a multitude of strategies and methods in reaching out to the rural areas. Broadly, these strategies include:

Strategies

Strategies	
reduction of poverty and hunger,	participatory appraisal and planning methodology
promotion of micro enterprises,	networking/federation methodologies
technology dissemination and transfer	community organisation
education – Formal, Non-formal and value education	supplementary, non-formal
skill building	*shramdhan*
training	community interaction
counselling	camps
attitudinal change	relief operations
awareness	cultural programme
infrastructure creation/maintenance	demonstrations
social mobilisation	exhibitions
management of CBOs and	rallies/processions
conflict resolution	*melas*
	film shows
	street plays
	trekking and
	campaigns

Rural Microsoft

Teachers of Sociology had in the past, taken their Master's students to nearby villages and taught them Rural

Sociology in the midst of villagers and rural environment. Currently, every student of sociology is attached to five families in a service village. During their extension hours, they are in regular contact with these families and facilitate development through awareness creation, family counselling, school enrollment and availing government programmes. The students are assessed for their extension activities every semester, based on the index of progress facilitated by the students.

Masters of Rural Project Management in the Department of Extension Education analysed the situation of a service village through Participatory Rural Appraisal (PRA) method, prioritised the problems and a pair of students took up a problem of their choice for an indepth study, preparation of an Action plan, and follow up till they succeeded or failed in solving the chosen problem. They took the people with them in meeting the BDOs, Bankers, Electricity Board Officials, Forest Officers, Revenue Officials or NGOs as warranted by the problem selected by the respective teams. This was labelled as Rural Microsoft i.e. Solution Oriented Field Training (SOFT) at the micro level in a rural area.

Students of Masters in Home Science from the Department of Home Science had taken up a delicate task of following up the progress made by chronic alcoholic patients, after a 10 day de-addiction camp at Gandhigram through T.T.K. Hospital, Chennai. Every student was given the responsibility of following up one alcoholic patient periodically, by providing necessary medicines and counseling to the patient as well as his family members.

Problems

Faculties and departments implementing extension programmes in their rural environs have reported to be confronted with the following problems:

1. Lack of field staff, transportation facilities, financial support, and documentation support for undertaking regular extension programmes
2. Difficulties in purchase of Science kits for schools and delay in release of funds from the institute
3. Lack of follow up of the extension activities by the departments
4. Clash of working hours for GRU students in their school teaching programme in villages
5. Permission from Education Department officials for school teaching programme for a period of 6 months or one year, instead of specific sessions
6. Marketing of products by rural women trained in mushroom cultivation.

Suggestions

GRU may consider the following suggestions for removing the thorns and thistles in the process of rural extension programmes:

1. People in villages are skeptical about change agents providing awareness on various issues. Therefore, 'Technical education' for capacity building of youth and adolescent girls and 'transfer of technology' to farmers, artisans and entrepreneurs should be the predominant components of our rural extension programmes.
2. GRU may acquire a vehicle with basic educational materials comprising science instruments and computers for teaching rural students regularly every evening and in week ends.
3. We may reorganise and rationalise the present system of use of Field staff, centralise it with Extension department, develop capacities of Field staff in select spheres of specialisation and deploy them in service village activities.

4. A renewed Rural Extension Policy may be evolved for implementation from 2007 for a period of five years. Ideas and suggestions from the faculty, field staff, students, village Panchayats, SHGs and stakeholders may be obtained in the process.
5. A Community Outreach Forum may be established in GRU with representatives from
   - Faculty and Field Staff
   - Final year Students
   - Community based people's organisations (SHGs, Panchayats)
   - Public Service Institutions (Schools, Health centres, Cooperatives and Banks)
   - Non-Government Organisations operating in the service areas
   - Government departments (Block and village levels)

   This forum may meet every three months and review the progress, perils and prospects of extension programmes and build up people-friendly programmes.
6. GRU has an Academic Council and a Research Advisory Committee for discussing teaching and research programmes. It has a Finance Committee, Syndicate and Senate for specific purposes, but none to deal with extension component. An Extension Advisory Council may therefore be set up immediately on a pioneering basis. In fact, UGC may insist on such a council for all the colleges and universities.
7. While UGC advocates the three pronged approach of teaching, research and extension in higher education, it should also allocate a certain percentage of the total budget towards rural extension activities. To begin with, it may be put at 25 per cent. GRI may set a trend by allocating even more i.e. 30 per cent, as its strength lies in the extension programmes.

Chapter 10

Institutional Linkage Programme for Village Development-Strengths and Weeknesses

K. Mahendrakumar,
R. Arunachalam and L. Nirmala

Origin of the programme

It is mandatory for the ICAR (Indian Council of Agriculture Research) and SAU's (State Agriculture Universities) involve in research, education and extension. In the context of the extension activities, ICAR formulated many outreach programmes starting from National Demonstration to ATIC (Agriculture Technology Information Centre). On the line of ICAR guidelines, the SAUs' also involved in many of those outreach programmes. Apart from this the SAUs also form a regional oriented extension programmes to serve the poor peasants. During 1998-99 one such regional oriented- linkage based programmes was started by Tamil Nadu Agricultural University viz., Integrated Village Development Programme (IVDP).

Under this Programme, the eight constituent colleges and 33 research stations of this university have to choose atleast two potential revenue villages in a radius of 10 km every year. In those selected villages the technical aspects of the research findings have to be spread through different ways of communication. Further, the scientists has to find out the problems existing in those villages pertinent to crop cultivation and clear farmers' doubts during their subsequent visits. It was decided in this programme that only technical guidance can be provided by the universities but no other support in kind or cash form. For organising the meetings, the expenditure has to be met by the villagers themselves.

As this is an integrated programme, it is expected to cover different aspects of village life such as health, sanitation, credit facilities, animal husbandry, etc. The technical persons required for operating this programme are drawn from different departments agricultural institutes and also from other development departments such as animal husbandry, sericulture, horticulture, banks, etc. The extension department in the agricultural institutes is a coordinating and implementing agent for this programme, which is expected to convene a meeting once in a fortnight in each village with the help of local leaders. The propaganda about the meetings can be conveyed to the common people through *'tom tom'* or through the common notice boards existing in panchayat union office. One such programmes was implemented by Madurai Agricultural College and Research Institute in three villages of Dindigul and Theni districts, located near Periakulam Horticultural College (Alagarnaikenpatti and Vazhayathupatti in the plains and Thadiankudisai Horticulture Research Station (Kaviakadu, a hill station village

Methodologies of outreach

Alagarnaickenpatti village is situated near the Horticultural College, and people from this village have been working as labourers in the college, who acted as a bridge between the community and students. In order to attract the attention of the farmers, cultural programmes oriented towards agricultural technologies were staged by the organisers with the help of students in the village. After gaining sufficient familiarity with the people, the scientists visited the village once in a fortnight in the evenings to have an interaction with the farmers and local leaders. Under NSS programme, the students also organised varied programmes. Once in a month, the officials, belonging to other development departments were encouraged to visit this village by organising a meeting.

Alagarnaickenpatti village, near horticulture college and Research Institute, Periyakulam consists of 500 households, of whom, 75 per cent of the population are involved in agricultural activities. Nearly 50 per cent of the farmers are having a landholding less than 2.5 acres. The major crops being cultivated in this area are sugarcane, paddy, cotton and some vegetables. It is having equal share of population of backward and scheduled caste community. They are living in harmony with each other. However, the people belong to scheduled caste are either a small farmer or a landless labourer who served in the field of backward community.

By considering the lack of resources, particularly technical manpower in the Horticultural research station, Thadiyankudisai (a hill station) only one village was selected under this programme. Here too, visits were made in the village once in a fortnight by the scientists of HRS. People were encouraged to visits the HRS in general, particularly during the seminar, workshop organised in this station. The neighbouring institutes such as Coffee Board, Spices Board were also involved in this programme to provide technical inputs and other subsidy oriented programmes.

Performance of the Programme

In the plains, in spite of involvement of students, scientists and officials of other development departments, people's participation was found to be lower. Most of the times, the organisers found it difficult to mobilise the people for the meetings though the local leaders were involved in this process. The major reasons attributed for the non-participation was that this programme promised only the technical information input but not any kind or subsidy.

technical information input but not any kind or subsidy. From the programmes of other development departments too, people had similar expectations but in vain.

Earlier, the meetings were organised during the office hours of the host institutes but to improve people's participation, as per the suggestions of the local leaders, the meetings were conducted during evening hours from 5 to 7 pm. Because of this change, the attention of farmers in this meetings increased marginally, with some hurdles though. It was found that during evenings, the farmers had the habit of taking liquor and attended the meeting. Under the influence of alcohol, they used to disturb the meetings. However, a few farmers who had good acquaintance with the students, visited the institutions frequently to get technical guidance for their field problems.

In the hill regions, the organisers found it difficult to conduct the meetings in the villages. It was difficult to find a suitable place for the gathering as this village is having lack of common facilities such as community halls and school buildings. Moreover, it was difficult to gather the farmers in the mornings. As there is a frequent shower and chillness in this hill region, it posed difficulties in conducting the meeting in the evening hours too. Moreover, there was frequent power cut which put additional burden on the organisers to conduct the meeting with all these difficulties, the organisers contacted the farmers fortnightly, with the help of local leaders. During such visits, the farmers were encouraged to visit the research stations. In spite of all these hurdles, participation of the people from this hillside village was found to be better than in the plains. By the initiative of the organisers, the people gained the knowledge of cultivation of vanilla crop and started cultivating them in their field on a trial basis.

The impact study carried out in this area revealed that the farmers gained technical advice on plant protection and cultivation of vanilla. In many meetings, the planters expressed that they required credit facilites to take up commercial agricultural business. In this regard, a meeting was organised in the village with the help of bank officials and they explained how they can get the crop loan. Through this programme, they had contact with the bank and the farmers got crop loan for cultivation of hill banana and vanilla.

Lessons learned

As the farmers were given subsidy from State Agriculture and Horticulture departments for more than two decades, they had the habit of demanding subsidy from all development programmes implemented for the welfare of the farmers. They had demanded wages for attending meetings meant for their welfare though. The village linkage programmes were not able to penetrate into the rural population with the technical component alone; instead, it required material and monetary component too for effective implementation.

Conceptually, linking up all the activities of the development departments under one umbrella in the name of integrated village development programmes sounds good but in reality, either a meaningful linkage or any integration in the activities of development department is hardly achieved. This is happening because every development department has its own set of programmes to be implemented within their own schedule. Hence, necessary cooperation and coordination required for implementing such programme could not be obtained from other development departments. In order to overcome this barrier, it is necessary to establish an independent coordinating machinery to take up such programmes with due recognition to every development department involved in it.

Chapter 11

Children: Can they be Change Agents?

A. Suriakanthi

Though most of us thought about how men, women and youth can be good change agents, not many have dared to ask whether children can be change agents. However, some interesting experiments and practices here and there have shown that children too can be effective change agents.

Who is a Change Agent?

A change agent is defined as some one who intentionally or indirectly causes or accelerates social, cultural or behavioural change.[1] Some definitions stress that the changes are to be different from the traditional way of handling or thinking about a problem.[2]

Why are Children important?

Children can influence changes in the society because of their uniqueness. First of all, unlike adults, all children are eager to learn. Because of eagerness, they are quick to acquire new knowledge. What children learn is likely to be followed throughout their life as they are deeply set in their mind. As they are the future parents and grand parents, they can cause or accelerate changes in the society.

By nature, children want to be engaged in some activity or other. Hence, skills can be taught to them easily. Such skills as are necessary for social change can be taught to them easily. As their minds are clear like a blank slate, their attitude can also be influenced.

Children have great influence on their parents. Parents love them and have a tendency to satisfy their wants and desires within reasonable limits. Hence, when they demand that certain of the conditions need to be changed, parents may yield. For example, when a child asks for a pair of *chappal,* in all likelihood, parents buy them for their children. Another way that children influence adults is that they pass on the knowledge and skills they acquire at school to their parents. Their influence is greater, especially when the parents are uneducated. There have been instances of children imparting literacy to parents.

Children have an appeal for other elders also. If they, as a group, demand something from adults, in all likelihood, they may get their demands fulfilled. In Burkina Faso, children under a Child – to – Child Project, could get a play ground for themselves from the community through their collective effort.

Children have a lot of time at their disposal. After school hours, they can spend a little of their time for community activities.

Children have a lot of artistic potential. They can influence and convince others througn their talents. They can sing, dance and role play. These talents may be focused on a development theme to the advantage of development activists / practitioners. They feel proud if they are involved in public activities and are delighted when their contribution is acknowledged and appreciated. This tendency of children can also be used for beneficial activities.

Children can be good change agents as they have a better sense of ownership and participation in public activities.[3] Children have been found to enjoy being members of student cabinets, and holding responsibilities like ministers of education, culture, sports, etc. They have been found to enjoy activities such as survey, workshops and practicals such as digging soak pits.[4]

Research Findings

A number of research studies have proved that children can be effective change agents. Fors and others (1989)[5] for example, studied the effectiveness of children as health messengers. They found that children were effective in different kinds of efforts such as promoting health awareness on hypertension and heart diseases. Similarly, the National Autonomous University of Honduras found that children were more effective in changing the hygiene practices of their family members than the health promoters (IDRC, 1990).[6] In another experiment, child siblings acted as change agents for promoting the functional status of the children with cerebral palsy. When children were taught about cerebral palsy, they could effect some behavioural change in the afflicted children (Craft *et al.* 1990).[7]

David, (2002)[8] reported that children were effective change agents in making parents take increased quantity of fruits and vegetables. In the area of environmental sustainability also, children have acted as change agents. London Sustainability Exchange (2006)[9] reports about an experiment in which children were effective agents of behaviour changes among their family members and members of their community towards greener life styles. Similarly, Nicotera (2007)[10] reports about a project wherein children were trained as agents of neighbourhood change. The ultimate aim was to change the civil society through these children.

Similarly, in a child – to – adult programme, children aged 5-10 were equipped with knowledge on AIDS through toys and stories and they acted as pressure group for their parents. More parents changed their behaviour due to educational intervention by children (Matsiko and Twinomujuni, 1996).[11]

In India, a number of projects related to social change have rested their belief on the premise that children are effective change agents. A project called "Project Citizen" in Kochi, Kerala has successfully mobilised children as resources for a social awareness programme towards the objective of bringing about positive social change (Balachandran, 2006).[12]

Based on her experiment with children as change agents, Sukanya Subramanian (2007)[13] of UNICEF India, has this to say: Our experience at UNICEF reveals that children are the best change agents at home and in the community. We believe that if we teach the children, they will in turn bring change in the family and thereby the entire community. This statement amply illustrates the importance of children as change agents.

A Rural University's Experience

The Gandhigram Rural University in Tamil Nadu, had an opportunity to work on the premise that children can be good change agents. Experiences of two projects have given valuable insights into children's potential as change agents. The first one has been the children's clubs.

Children's Clubs: In the 1960s, Children's Clubs were started in 13 villages, where 13 child care centres were functioning. Since then, activities have been going on for the past 40 years. So far, roughly 10,400 children have been active members of children's club during these years.

Children's Club members have been involved in group activities such as cleaning the premises of the village, group study, group reading, village library activity, preparing drama on themes of rural development and teaching literacy to parents, etc.

A commendable activity by the club, which is crucial for change, is persuading parents and their non-enrolled children to go to school. In Indian villages, children drop out at various grades owing to poverty, lack of motivation, poor conditions in the school, etc. Children's Club members identify children who are not likely to go to school (when the school re-opens) and persuade such children and the parents to send these children to school. The impact of such activity is very significant.

Being members of Children's Club makes them stand apart among from their peers. What differentiates them from others is a sense of discipline, oneness and eagerness to help others. These children, having been exposed to group activities and group training are more sociable than the others. They know the acceptable ways of interacting with elders. They are willing to share their group's savings with the poor amongst them, the aged and destitutes in their community. Children's Club members of Kallupatti, a village near Gandhigram, bought books and stationery for their fellow students. They gave rice for a poor old man who had no one to take care of. The adults were highly appreciative of the social activities of these children and encouraged their own children to become club members. When the children gathered to clean their village, adults also joined hands with the children. Thus, Children's Club members have influenced the sanitation and nutrition practices and literacy of their parents.

The experiences with children's club have given certain valuable hints. Some of them are:

1. Children of age 13, 14 and 15 years can devote considerable time for community activities. Those who are to appear for final exams at the 10th and 12th Standards are unable to give adequate time for community activities.
2. Evening time would be ideal for group activities, especially, between 6 p.m. and 7.p.m. Children come back from school by 5 p.m. and after finishing their household chores, they can devote some time for community improvement.
3. Devoting time on all days will not be possible for children. Hence, Saturdays will be ideal. Children can spend their time in public activities on Saturdays.

4. Children do not expect any monetary returns for their activities. They are motivated by the benefits / results of their activity to the community. A word of praise or a pat on their back is a sufficient reward for them.

Child-to-Child Project: The second major experiment with children in GRU was the "Child-to-Child Project" funded by the Bernard van Leer Foundation of the Netherlands. The Child-to-Child experiment of Gandhigram Rural University in 25 schools of Athoor block of Dindigul District has proved that children could be good family and community educators in nutrition and sanitation.

Child-to-child is an international network promoting children's participation in health and development. It is situated at the University of London's Institute of Education. Child–to–child approach is an educational activity. It links children's learning with taking action to promote the health, well-being and development of themselves, their families and communities" (Child–to–Child Trust, 2006).[14]

The experiment in GRU was carried out in two stages. The first one was to enlighten the children of the 5th standard on the basics of nutrition and sanitation. For a good change agent, right knowledge, attitude and skills are essential. For example, if a child has to be a good change agent in sanitation, he/she must know the basics of sanitation, the skills related to sanitation practices and the right attitude related to sanitation. Hence, at the initial stage itself, these volunteers were equipped with the necessary knowledge through stories, games and role play. The Child-to-child activity sheets prepared and distributed by the child-to-child Trust were extensively used. These activity sheets have been prepared by experts, suitably illustrated and are full of learning by doing activities.

Having thus empowered, these children initially started on community education. This is the second stage of the experiment. They enacted street plays which attracted a big crowd, generally in front of their school.

These children did not stop with teaching their communities. They started educating their parents too. They wanted their parents to buy them chappals so that they would not suffer worm infestations. They asked their mothers to cook greens as the greens were rich sources of vitamins and minerals.

Moreover, as the care takers of the younger ones at home, they provided play activities and imparted good health habits to their siblings.

Yet another strategy was that the older children were paired with younger ones at school. For instance, the children of 5th standard were paired with the children of 1st standard. The older ones monitored the cleanliness of the younger ones. They monitored the health practices of younger children such as taking bath, keeping their head free of lice, cutting nails and using toilet for defecation.

Conclusion

The narration so far shows that extension educators, rural development practitioners and researchers have tried to harness child power for improving the quality of life of people, particularly those in rural areas. It also shows that the problems in rural areas, particularly, those of malnutrition, ill health, poor sanitation and water management and illiteracy can be effectively tackled with the active involvement of children. Towards this, the first step is to empower them with the necessary basic knowledge in nutrition, health and sanitation. Budgetary provision has to be made by governments for providing non-formal education to children on the essential facts of healthy living. This should be an essential basic component of education for all. Reaching the Millennium Development Goals will certainly be accelerated by equipping and involving children as educators. A seed sown at the right time in the right soil will certainly sprout. Children educated at the right time, in the proper way, will certainly blossom into powerful change agents.

Reference

1. Wikipedia (2006). Change Agent. http.en.wikipedia.org/wiki/change-agent.
2. Barron's Educational Services, Inc (2000). Dictionary of Business Terms. www.answers.com/topic/change agent.
3. WASTE, (2007). Children as Agents of Change. http:/ www.ecosan.nl./page/910.
4. UNICEF (2006). Making Children the Change Agents. www.unicef.org/india/child protection 2438./htm.
5. Fors & Others quoted by David, M. *et al.*, (2002). Using Children as Change Agents to Increase Fruit and Vegetable Consumption among Lower Income African American Parents. http://www.ars.usda.gov/research/publication./publicaitons.htm?seq.no_115=172117.
6. International Development Research Centre, (2006). Children as Change Agents(Honduras).www.Idrc.Ca/En/Ev-67579-201 8060225 1 Idrc Adm. Info.Html.
7. Craft *et al.*, (1990). Siblings as Change Agents for Promoting the Functional Stages of Children with Cerebral Palsy. www.ncbi.nlm.gov/sites/entrez?cmd= Retrieved db= pubMed and list uids = 22863038d dept.=abstract.
8. David, M. *et al.*, *op. cit.*
9. London Sustainability Exchange, (2006). Children as Change Agents. http.//www.lsx.orguk/whatwedo/CACA page2664.aspx.
10. Nicotera, N. (2007). Building Skills for Civic Engagement: Children as Agents of Neighbourhood Change. http:/sswr./confex.com/sswr/2007/techprogrammes/p6070.Htm.

11. Matsiko, B, & Twinomujuni, N.K. (1996). The Impact of Children's Effort on Behaviour Change. http:/ gateway.nlm.nik.gov./MectryAbstracts/ 10221685.html.

12. Balachandran, S., (2006). Children as Change Agents. www.hinduonnet.com/thehindu/mp/2006/05/ 29stories/2006/052900790300.htm.

13. Subramanian, S., (2008). Making Children the Change agents. www.unicef.org/India/was_2438_htm.

14. Child–to–Child, (2006). http.//www.child-to-child.org.

Chapter 12

Children's Participation and Right – based Approaches

"You don't have to be old to be wise"

T. Rajkumar

Non-Governmental Organisations (NGOs) often intervene in situations where social conditions have deteriorated and the available resources cannot bring about lasting positive changes. Instead of trying to cure social crises, there is need to build a society capable of "preventing" these breakdowns altogether. We believe that this can be accomplished by influencing future decision makers, such as children, and by enabling them to make socially responsible decisions.

Working with children is challenging and rewarding at the same time. It requires immense patience and unwavering trust and energy, but on the other hand, the experience offers enormous satisfaction, and re-energises and re-establishes one's future.

It is commonly supposed that the UN Convention on the Rights of the Child provides clear engagement for children's participation. The CRC provides a new vision of children. It brings together the familiar view of the child "as a venerable human being that requires protections and assistance from the family, the society and the State" with the perception that he/she is a subject of right who is able to form and express opinions, to participate in decision-making processes and influence solution, to intervene as a partner in the process of social change in the building up of democracy (Santos Pais, 1999:4).

The paragraphs of the CRC usually cited as explicit support for children's participation are as follows:

1. State parties shall assure to the child who is capable of forming his or her own views, the right to express those views freely in all matters affecting the child and the views of the child being given due weight in accordance with age and maturity of the child
2. For this purpose, the child shall in particular be provided with the opportunity to be heard in any judicial and administrative proceedings affecting the child, either directly, or through a representative or appropriate body, in manner consistent with the procedural rules of national law.

- Article 12 of the UN Convention on Rights of the Child.

Adults as well as children approach the relationships with a certain degree of caution because there are several pre-conceived notions about each other that could result in conflicts.

The conflicting perception

According to adults, children....	According to children, adults are....
• Lack commitment	• Too demanding
• Are self absorbed	• Unwilling to give personal space
• Are undisciplined	• Regiment lists
• Are not interested in	• Oblivious to hear and now realities
• Are a Long-term plan	• Not interested in the emotional aspects and are temperamental
• Lack experience	• Not ready to give chances
• Only want to have fun	• Straight- jacketed and boring

It is accepted that there is some truth in what both parties have to say. However, we believe that it is possible to work around these perceptions if we as a team of adults take on the onus of taking the first step. In the process, we must also ensure that children also change their stances, attitudes, and behaviour.

The Nature of Participatory Processes

Generally speaking, there are five types of contexts where children's participation occurs in a deliberate and organised way:

1. Events held at local, national, regional and international level in which children are encouraged to voice their concerns.
2. Participatory research undertaken in direct relation to agency's programmes
3. Child-led initiative, such as clubs and children's parliament, usually at the local level
4. Community development projects in which children are involved together with adults.
5. Social and work-related movements/ organisations such as associations of child workers or street children

Different types of activities are undertaken with general hopes of improving children's lives.

A. Conceptualising Children's participation

Basic understanding

Participatory programming needs to be accompanied by organisation-wide understanding of the definitions of children's participation, it's aims and the methodologies involved.

Recognising limits, defining boundaries of children's participation

Important to articulate a clear position with regard to the areas and extent of engagement, particularly in sensitive issues that may have political implications such as child labour.

Developing an holistic approach

Participatory project needs to be part of a broad vision for the development and improvement of the situation of children within the country as a whole and children's participation should be an operating principle that is mainstreamed across the entire country.

Knowledge of working context

Understanding of context on the part of implementing agencies is necessary in order to anticipate and overcome the kind of obstacles like the negative attitudes of adult community members that may lie in the way of participatory projects.

B. Facilitation of Children's Participatory Project

Quantity and quality of facilitation

Facilitating children's participation requires sustained and sometimes intensive interaction between children and adults, and thus it is important to have sufficient dedicated staff.

Long – term and ongoing training for facilitators

Staff need to be well – trained, well supported with a progressive vision and strategies for children's participation in community development.

Selection of suitable facilitators

Need to consider what kinds of people are suitable as facilitator. For example, volunteer teachers may use similar methods to facilitate participatory projects as they do in the classroom, which is geared predominantly towards preparing students for national examination by imparting fixed sets of information through rote learning.

Use of volunteer facilitators

Need to consider to what extent volunteers can take part in training initiative and commit themselves to sustained support of children's participatory projects.

Provision of dedicated space for project

The provision of space that is set aside and guaranteed for project participation to meet and conduct activities is of great importance and adults should assist children to attain the material conditions that they required.

Selection of suitable location

Agencies should consider the general atmosphere of a location and whether it is conducive to participation, is inclusive rather than exclusive, is readily accessible and comfortable for all children.

C. Organisational Culture and Corporate Requirements

Participatory approaches and organisational culture

Participation is likely to be achieved only when democratic, participatory approaches are institutionalised, or mainstreamed throughout an organisation as a whole. Senior staff should be involved with children on a regular basis.

Funding

Need to consider the conditions that different sources of funding, grants or sponsorship, create for children's participation, either enabling or hindering.

Monitoring and evaluation systems

Need for adequate staff to implement good quality participatory projects as well as to meet the administrative, monitoring and evaluation and requirements of sponsorship and grants.

CHILD PARTICIPATION

MYTH AND REALITY

Myth: Child Participation means choosing one child to represent children's perspectives and opinions in an adult forum.

Reality: Children are not a homogeneous group, and no one child can be expected to represent the interests of their peers of different ages, races, ethnicities and gender. Children need forums of their own in which they can build skills, identify their priorities, communicate in their own way and learn from their peers. In this way, children are better able to make their own choices as to who should represent their interests and in what ways they would like their viewpoints presented.

Myth: Child participation involves adults handing over all their power to children who are not ready to handle it.

Reality: Participation does not mean that adults simply surrender all decision making power to children. The Convention on the Rights of the Child (CRC) is clear that children should be given more responsibility – according to their evolving capacities as they develop. In many cases adults still make the final decision, based on the best interest of the child – but with the CRC in mind, it should be a decision informed by the views of the child. As children grow older, parents are to allow them more responsibility in making decisions that affect them – even those that may be controversial, such as custody matters following a divorce.

Myth: Children should be children, are not to be forced to take on responsibilities that should be given to adults.

Reality: Children should certainly be allowed to be children, and to receive all the protection necessary to safeguard their healthy development. And no child should be forced to take on responsibilities for which they are not ready. But children's healthy development also depends upon being allowed to engage with the world, making more independent decisions and assuming more responsibility as they become more capable. Children who encounter barriers to their participation may become frustrated or even apathetic; 18 year-olds without the experience of participation will be poorly equipped to deal with the responsibilities of democratic citizenship.

Myth: Child participation is merely a sham. A few children, usually from an elite group, are selected to speak to powerful adults who then proceed to ignore what the children say while claiming credit for listening to kids.

Reality: Children's participation, in many instances, has proven to be very effective. Rather than setting up an ineffectual system, it is up to all of us to devise meaningful forms of children's participation that benefit them and, in turn, society as a whole.

Myth: Child participation actually only involves adolescents, who are on the verge of adulthood anyway.

Reality: The public, political face of children's participation is more likely to be that of an adolescent than a 6-year-old, but it is essential to consult children of all ages about the issues that affect them. This means participation within schools and families, when decisions about matters there are being discussed. At every age, children are capable of more than they are routinely given credit for – and will usually rise to the challenges set before them if adult support their efforts.

Myth: No country in the world consults children on all the issues that affect them and no country is likely to do so soon.

Reality: That's partly true. However, all countries that have ratified the Convention on the Rights of the Child have committed themselves to ensuring participation rights for children, e.g., the rights to freely express their views on matters that affect them and to freedom of thought, conscience, religion, association and peaceful assembly. And almost every country can now show significant advances in setting systems and policies in place to allow children to exercise these rights.

Myth: Children may be consulted as a matter of form but their views never change anything.

Reality: Where children's views are sensitively solicited and sincerely understood, they often change a great deal; they may reveal things that adults would never have grasped independently, they can profoundly change policies or programmes and in some cases, protect children from future harm. The consultation of even very young children can produce remarkable results. The problem is that such careful consultation of children remains rare.

Myth: Children's refusal to participate negates their rights.

Reality: Actually, resistance itself can be an important part of participation. Whether in the give and take of the home, in the refusal to accept punishment at school, or in one's attitude towards civic engagement in the community, resistance can signal a children's or adolescent's opinion about an issue or feeling about the terms of their involvement. Adults should recognize resistance as a form of communication and respond to it through understanding, dialogue and negotiation, rather than by trying to prevent it through force or persuasion. In no situation, should children be forced to participate.

Source

The states of the world's children –2003

What works in youth participation?

Foreword by Rick Little

International youth foundation

Understanding and evaluating children's participation

A review of contemporary literature – October – 2003

For Plan UK/Plan International

Chapter 13

Environmental Education for Rural Children – Approaches and Methodologies

R. Bhanumathi

Introduction

Our environment comprises air, water, earth, plants and animals that are extremely important for the existence of life on this planet. The components of environment are interlinked and man depends on these elements for his existence. All life forms are interdependent and play an important role in keeping our eco-system alive. Due to man's greed, our natural resources are depleting at an alarming rate. Due to population explosion, excessive urbanisation and with attendant pollution, we are facing environmental problems of great magnitude. This makes conservation and environmental protection an urgent need for the survival of mankind. Many international organisations have drawn attention to the need for long-term environmental policies to achieve any form of sustainable development. The Constitution of India Article 51 A g states:

It shall be the duty of every citizen to protect and improve the natural environment including forests, lakes, rivers and wildlife and to have compassion for living creatures.

Need and Scope

Good air, good water and good soil form the basis of a healthy environment and are essential for life to continue. These building blocks of life must be cared, preserved and enhanced. Education and awareness are the prime effective forces towards saving our besieged environment. Education makes people aware of the need for any activity and can generate the much-needed support for the success of the activity.

Environmental Education has many meanings. Some perceive it as preparation of people for their lives as members of the biosphere. Environmental Education is both theoretical and practical as it is `learning how to manage and improve the relationship between human society and the environment in an integrated and sustainable way'. Environmental Education is also perceived as –

- Learning experience gained from the environment in the form of skill development, investigation and enquiry, communication and cooperative problem solving.
- Education about the environment includes a basic knowledge and understanding of environmental processes (atmospheric, hydrologic, geomorphic and ecological) and concepts (water conservation, soil erosion, green house effect, habitat destruction, etc.). Knowledge about human environmental behaviour is an essential component of environment education.
- Education for environment encourages behaviors that are environmentally sustainable, and helps to ensure that future producers and decision makers demonstrate sensitivity towards environment.

The Belgrade Charter, written in 1975 by world experts in environmental education, mentions that the goal of Environmental Education is to:

Develop a citizenry that is aware of and concerned about the total environment and its associated problems and that has the knowledge, attitudes, motivations, commitments and skills to work individually and collectively towards solutions of current problems and preventions of new ones.

Role of Environmental Education

Environmental Education is fundamental to the future well being of the planet and its inhabitants. Individual and social use of the environment happens through the exploration and development of insights, awareness, knowledge, skills and attitudes. Environmental Education enables young people to understand, analyze and evaluate the relationship between people and their surroundings. This is achieved through an understanding of the ecological processes that govern life on earth; an understanding of the geomorphic and climatic patterns that influence living things and human activity; an understanding of the social and cultural influences that determine human values, perceptions and behaviour; and awareness of an individual's personal relationship with the environment as a consumer, producer and a member of society.

Environmental Education and National Policy on Education

Admiration and appreciation of nature and the urge to conserve and protect it has been part of our civilisation from time immemorial. Our ancestors were environmentally conscious. They advocated and practiced concepts of sustained usage of resources through many social customs, myths, taboos, traditions and religion.

Rural people everywhere have a good perception of their surrounding natural system, and a deep reverence for the systems. They have passed down both their understanding and their reverence, carefully from generation to generation through oral communication. However, the underlying reasons for doing so and the ways of doing so have changed over time.

The National Policy on Education (NPE) - a major initiative in the field of education by the Government of India was formulated in 1986, after a decade of study and experimentation. Article 8.15 of this policy concerns education and environment, which proclaims, There is a paramount need to create a consciousness of the environment. It must permeate all ages and all sections of society beginning with the child. Environmental consciousness should inform teaching in schools and colleges. This aspect should be integrated in the entire educational process.

By this mandate, Environmental Education has become an integral part of the educational development from pre-primary to higher education in India, where educational institutions are actively involved in translating the above policy into curriculum, textbooks and teacher training progammes and materials for all types and levels of education. The Policy thus stressed the need for equipping children with better knowledge, attitudes, values and skills to face and live with the world around us and to adjust to the changing conditions of the society. As today's children are tomorrow's citizens, responsible for the healthy growth of environment and society at all levels, there is a need to provide proper input through Environmental Education.

Rural Children and Environmental Education

The first serious attempt at relating education in the schools to local environmental needs was launched by Mahatma Gandhi as basic education movement. The elements of basic education were productive activity in education, correlation of the curriculum with productive activity and the physical and social environment and intimate contact between the school and the local community.

The rural school has two types of teaching – the formal one based on the curriculum and academic related and the non-formal type based on learning and doing things with joy and fun. Formal school education in rural India itself, in general, has not progressed much due to lack of physical facilities and infrastructure, single teacher schools, low teacher-student proportion, teacher nominated instruction, irregularity in teaching and teacher attendance, lack of in-service teacher education and low motivation levels of the teaching community. This situation can be seen even today in most of the remote rural areas all over India while some rural schools have achieved marginal progress due to the awareness programmes and influence of local voluntary organisations and Non-governmental Organisations (NGO). Kumar (2005) reveals the sordid reality of rural schooling in India. He writes that millions of village children are not able to complete eight years of elementary education and those who complete have limited chance of clearing class X and XII examinations. An NGO report has estimated that out of every 100 village girls enrolling in class I, just one survives in the system to reach class XII. Thus, incorporation of Environmental Education in the formal teaching process may not be the right solution. However, an attempt through non-formal education, which the NGOs have been successfully implementing in many Indian villages since eighties, appears to be a better option.

Approaches to Environmental Education

The approaches planned for rural Environmental Education should include the following aspects:

- location-specific issues
- cater to capacities and skills of the teacher
- planned according to the availability of low cost teaching aids like flip charts, flannel boards, posters, and charts. They should also include traditional communication media like folk songs, street plays, and puppetry that are people oriented communication methods for effective and long lasting dissemination of messages.
- themes or concepts selected should include traditional use and practices in the field of agriculture, grain storage, conservation of sacred groves, bio-diversity conservation including food crops, forests and wildlife.

Role of Rural School Teachers

School teachers play a vital role in imparting knowledge in Environmental Education in rural schools. Teacher should be able to develop in students a sense of awareness of themselves and their environment and to develop the basic observation skills through questions and discussions. The students should be given sensory experience like looking, observing, handling, feeling, listening, smelling, and tasting. Teachers as motivators must encourage behaviours, which are environmentally sustainable. The teachers can cultivate in their students curiosity, interest and respect for themselves and their world. The attempts and contribution for a better environment by students should be valued and appreciated in a positive way. With the help of teachers, activity oriented Environmental Education concepts may be practiced as suggested by Yomi Noibi, (1991) an African Environmental Educationist. He states that:

Learning to be environmentally literate comes through `doing something' for the environment and not just through learning about the environment.

The following strategies and approaches may be adopted by teachers for effective implementation of Environment Education concepts and themes.

Conducting Awareness Programmes

Teachers may initiate awareness programmes in the form of exhibitions, rallies, seminars, *padyatras,* film and slide shows, in schools, to spread the message of nature conservation and related topics to fulfill the aims of Environmental Education.

Preparation of Educational Programmes

To make the learning process interesting and innovative educative materials in the form of flash cards, flip charts, posters, charts, models, handouts and puppets may be prepared by the teachers.

Skill Development Activities

The teachers may ask students to express their ideas about environment through drawing and painting, *rangoli*, poster and chart making, model and wall paper preparation, bark and leaf prints, nature scrap books, collage making, music and dance, drama, skits, street plays, debates, oratory, group discussion, quizzes, story telling, poem-recitation, essay writing, puppet shows, etc. There is greater participation in any activity-oriented programme, which involves creativity in some form or other. Creativity also gives tremendous scope for self-expression, which is important for developing individual skills.

Formation of Clubs

The school authorities may initiate formation of Nature clubs, Eco clubs, green clubs and other similar clubs and associate with NGOs promoting these kind of outreach activities in rural schools. This way a sustained interest on Environment Education may be created. The club members may take part in field activities, nature oriented camps organised in wildlife sanctuaries, national parks and other wilderness areas, project work, tree planting, rallies, campaigns, competitions, seminars, animal census operation work with forest department, preparation of flora fauna checklist and other activities organised by NGOs. The participation of rural children in these Environmental Education activities encourages them to take up larger issues at a later stage in their lives. Some activities like tree planting help the entire community to increase the green cover.

Thus, Environmental Education not only makes the present generation aware of their responsibilities towards the future but also makes successive generation to view the continuation of life on earth as one of the most central of all human values. The strategies and approaches planned for Environmental Education will ultimately result in sustained growth and development of a nation by keeping nature and bio-diversity alive.

Chapter 14

Child-centered Rural Outreach - Experiments by Home Science Students

S.Kavitha @ Maithily and N. Kamalamma

Life Skills

Extension is an educational activity which tries to transmit knowledge, wisdom and skills to the community. Extension work should be considered important not only in terms of service to the society but also as a learning device both for the teachers and the students in universities. Knowledge imparted to the students is relevant in the specific societal context and the students are exposed to the realities of life beyond the narrow classroom situation.

Actual observation and experience of social realities is often better than reading about them from a dozen books. It is through various forms of extension activities that the teacher is able to add this dimension of teaching and learning. It is important to establish integral links between institutions of higher learning and the community, leading to mutual advantage. The community benefits from the expertise available in such institutions and the teachers and students get better educated by learning from the community.

Extension work is a ground for experimentation of students' knowledge, skills and expertise in their field. While doing extension work, students acquire life skills which are essential for the betterment of life. Life skills are essentially those abilities that help promote mental well being and competence in young people as they face the realities of life. Intellectual competence alone is not sufficient to live effectively in this world.

Today's youth need training in acquiring psycho-social competence and establishing better interpersonal relationships. According to WHO, the most direct interventions for the promotion of psycho-social competence are those which enhance the person's coping resources and personal and social competencies – supportive learning environment.

Experiences

Gandhigram Rural University, renowned for its extension activities among the higher education institutions, believes in learning by doing and experiencing by performing. The Department of Home Science, one of the pioneering departments established during 1956 when the university was established as an Institute, has been carrying out various extension activities for the benefit of rural women and children. Health education, empowerment of rural women, empowerment of children, popularisation of drinking water and rural sanitation technologies, diabetes prevention education, and awareness on alcoholism are some of its outreach activities.

As part of its extension activities, final year Master's students, specialising in Home Science Extension, carried out child-centred extension activities in Ramanathapuram village, in Athoor Block of Dindigul district for a period of six months. This village was selected due to proximity to the university and familiarity to the department. It has a school with about 100 students and two teachers. The major activities carried out by the group of Gandhigram students could be classified as follows:

1. Edu-tainment Programmes

The school children of Ramanathapuram village could not develop on par with their neighbouring urban counterparts because of their poor family background. Their parents could hardly think of providing better education to their children and imparting desirable values. The students of Gandhigram University realised this condition during their regular village placement programmes. So they planned to visit the village thrice a week and teach the children especially certain tough subjects like English, Maths and Science subjects. Children attended the classes with interest and around twenty children benefited by this educational outreach' programme blended with entertainment.

Science education was imparted through an innovative and interesting mode. A magic show was organised to teach simple scientific concepts to high school children. The children were astonished to notice jasmine flowers inside the coconut, burning of a paper without fire, etc. Then they were taught about the scientific facts behind it. Their superstitious beliefs were thus got rid of.

Initially, the students provided supplementary education to school children as majority of them were from socially and economically deprived families. Along with supplementary education in difficult subjects, the students were also oriented in drawings, paper foldings, and handworks. While working with the children, the students identified that the children lacked personal hygiene, they had improper eating habits and were not exposed to art or craft works. So the students planned providing health and nutrition education through entertainment as their next extension activity.

The students showed much interest in planning this programme. They evolved their own games, wrote rhymes, stories, etc., to impart health and nutrition education to the children. This programme was welcomed by both the parents and teachers. Subsequently, remarkable changes were noticed in the food habits of the children during their lunch time in schools. They ate vegetables, avoided wastage of food and also maintained cleanliness in their dining halls. Parents also reported that their children were taking bath regularly and trying to keep their place neat. Some of the children demanded their parents to get shoes for them, although the poor parents could not afford. Hence the parents discouraged their wards in practicing expensive hygiene ideas.

2. *Learning through Natural Colour*

Arts is essential to every child's education. It is through art that the children start communicating their thoughts, wishes and feelings. Drawing and paintings are an excellent media to explore the creativity of children. But an exposure to art education or an opportunity for drawing and painting is not enjoyed by many of our rural children. Even though art was incorporated in the curriculum, many rural children could not enjoy the joy of drawings and paintings. In most situations, these students could not afford to buy colour pencils, sketches or water colours. An alternative to these materials was explored, which is either low cost or no cost.

In order to explore the creativity and provide an opportunity to draw and paint, naturally and locally available materials such as charcoal, red soil, leaves, flower, etc. were identified. The children enthusiastically collected all these materials, and were encouraged to draw on the old news papers initially. Charcoal was used for such drawing. Red soil was made into a paste by adding water. This paste was used for finger painting. Colours were also extracted from the leaves of hibiscus, *neem*, flowers like hibiscus, (Hibiscus rosa sinensis), *Sangupoo* (Clitoria ternate), *Kahithapoo* (Bougenville mohara), etc.

These colours are natural, harmless, attractive, economical and easily available. While working with these colours, the children profoundly expressed their joy and happiness. They could draw various imaginative pictures of their own. In the process, they could also learn about different plants. This exercise also stimulated their curiosity to know the other colour yielding plants in their location. Extraction and use of natural colours nurtured the creativity of both the students and rural children. They understood how to use the locally available resources and to plan programmes for the child's holistic development.

3. *Summer Joy*

Productive use of the children's time during summer vacation is the prime botheration of every parent. The Department of Home Science organised a 'Summer Joy programme' for school children from the neighbouring village schools, which provided opportunities to learn science in its style and setting. With a package of 120 contact hours, the programme comprised nature study/walk, role play, drama, creative learning exercises, free play, communication skills, project work, scientific experiments, and study tours. Home Science students served as volunteers in steering this programme which was organised during five consecutive summers since 2002. Parents expressed their happiness about this programme which, according to them, triggered the creativity of their children, improved their eating habits and systematised their daily routines.

Student volunteers who steered this programme informed that they gained skills in planning. Organising and co-ordinating children's programme. They improved their understanding of child behaviour through observation and interaction, motivating and managing children's group and developing in them skills such as negotiation, problem solving, etc. and gained leadership quality. As a significant outcome of their involvement in this programme, students got sensitised towards rural realities which would help them in planning and executing children's programmes systematically in future. This child outreach programme catered to on the one hand, the needs of rural children and fully exploited the untapped latent potentials of our students on the other.

4. *Community Service*

In order to find out the means to sustain various programmes initiated by the students, the team identified a local organisation. The SHG members were not found to be competent enough to handle the teaching component. Nor were there youth clubs in the village. The team, then planned to form a youth club in the village. Initially, it was difficult to meet the youth in the village during the day, since they were working in various places and their work hours differed. Due to day shifts, night shifts, migratory work, etc. it was difficult to organize them. After two months of struggle, a meeting was conducted among the village youth and finally, the students could succeed in getting the youth club registered. Educated and interested youth were engaged for providing supplementary education to the school children.

During one of their visits, the students identified a 12 year old child with mental retardation. The child regularly attended the school in order to get the mid-day meals. His parents were agricultural labourers and were not aware of the government schemes for the disabled. They were not prepared to sacrifice their wages and visit the government departments to enquire about schemes. Hence the students took up the responsibility of helping the boy. They visited the District Disabled Rehabilitation office at Dindigul district Collectorate and enquired about the various schemes available for the disabled and procedures in getting the same. With lot of hardships, the students could take the disabled child to the Government doctor and get him the much needed Disability identity card. With this card, they could get monthly pension for the boy from the government intended for the disabled children.

Learning Experience

The extension work carried out by the students may not bring about an immediate social change. But it acted as a major tool to develop sensitivity among the students and helped to build them as future social engineers. The students and teachers acquired certain lessons from these experiences some of these include:

- They acquired teaching skills while carrying out the educational outreach programme. It also motivated the students to prepare simple teaching aids.

- Learning science through magic show offered them knowledge through visuals. It cultivated the scientific temper among students.
- Using natural colours for drawing developed their creativity, increased their botanical knowledge and added to their creativity.
- The joyful learning programme developed the latent talents and skills of the students. They became writers, poets, and innovators.
- The students sharpened their communication skills while meeting the people, government officials, and school teachers.
- When working with heterogeneous people, the students' coping skills got strengthened and co-ordination was ensured while working as a team. (Some people co-operated while others hesitated).
- Children were attending the classes regularly for a while but disappeared after sometime. And hence they needed constant monitoring.
- The teachers and the community criticised their work in their own way, but the students and teachers coped up with all these ordeals with a smile.

Conclusion

Today's student is the responsible citizen of tomorrow. One of the important duties of our students is to devote themselves to service. They should realize that knowledge can be had through service too. Higher educational institutions should provide opportunities for the students to serve the needy and deprived people in the community in tune with their curriculum. Community outreach activities help for promotion of national consciousness among the youth. Besides developing socially responsible individuals, extension activities act as a chisel in sculpturing the personality of youth and it is the best medium to impart life skills to the students.

Reference

1. Montessori, Maria, (2006). **The Secret of Childhood.** Chennai: Orient Longman Pvt. Ltd.
2. Narayanasamy. N., Karthikeyan. G., & Thillainayagam. N. (Ed). (2004). **Rural Extension in Higher Education - the Experience of Gandhigram Rural University,** Gandhigram.
3. Pankajam, G., (2000). **Extension-Third Dimension of Education,** New Delhi: Gyan Publishing House.
4. Vinoba, (1959). **Thoughts on Education.** Akil Bharat Sarva Seva Sangh, New Delhi.
5. **The Progressive Social Role of a University Teacher.** (1991). ES – 301 Higher Education: its context and linkages. New Delhi: Indira Gandhi National Open University.

Chapter 15

Reaching out to the Tribal Women through Scientific and Development Interventions

A. Sakunthalai, R. Ganesan and K. Ramakrishnan

As long as women of India do not take part in public life there can be no salvation for the country.

- Mahatma Gandhi

Introduction

India is one of the largest democracies in the world. The Constitution of India bestows equal rights and opportunities to all its citizens. But women are deprived of equal opportunity in the patriarchal society of India.

Women are a vital part of the Indian economy constituting one-third of the national labour force and a major contributor to the survival of the family. Despite progress in several key indicators, a gender analysis of social and economic data demonstrates that women in India continue to be relatively disadvantaged in matters of survival, health, nutrition, literacy and productivity. Since 37 years of Independence, India stands today with a dismal record in social development sectors.

Two-thirds of all work is performed by women who constitute half the population but only share one-tenth of the income and one hundredth of the property (FAO, 1988). Studies on women in agriculture conducted in India reveal that by and large, women are found doing manual, low prestige, hazardous, arduous, monotonous, repetitive and time consuming jobs *viz.*, transplanting, picking, weeding, harvesting and processing.

At the same time, agricultural work is not free from hazards. In the case of women, these get aggravated mainly due to prevalence of higher levels of malnutrition, anaemia, parasitic infection, frequent child bearing, long hours of work and mishandling of agricultural tools and equipments.

In the words of Swaminathan (1988), despite women's importance to agricultural production, women face severe handicaps. They are in fact the largest group of landless labourers, with little real security in case of family break-up, inheritance laws, land reforms and family customs. Agricultural development programmes are usually planned by men and aimed at men, mechanisation to alleviate the burden of task that are traditionally men's responsibility leaving women's burden unrelieved and at times even increased. Extension workers, almost exclusively males, aim their advice at men, on men's activities and crops.

Even though several theoretical concepts and indices to measure empowerment of women have been identified and proposed worldwide, very few studies have been conducted empirically to measure 'women empowerment'. In the present study, a pioneering attempt has been made to develop a scale to measure women empowerment and this was applied through case study analysis.

The case study has been analysed with a broad spectrum of highlighting the empowerment of women with a significant view of not only reforming and refining their life towards the egalitarian society but also into the direction of economic achievement of the country. It is in this context, the farm women selected for the case study were categorised as very low, low, medium, high and very high based on the Women Empowerment Index (WEI) score. From the category of high to very high level of empowerment of the block, Tmt.Valliammal was selected as successful farm woman of Thondamuthur block. The information collected from the case study analysis is presented below.

Valliammal, W/o Perumal, aged 30, educated upto 8th standard lives with her husband aged 35, who is educated only upto 3rd standard. Her traditional occupation is farming. She belongs to tribal community, her family owned 1.5 acres of irrigated land which got irrigated from the river running through their area. Her village is located near the Velliangry hills and comprised 50 families.

She expressed that, in the earlier days, there were no schools, no facilities for drinking water, the houses were without permanent roof which was just made with teak leaves. There were no transport facilities, no communication facilities, no medical facilities. They were handicapped in availing the basic infrastructure facilities. She was unaware of improved farm implements and technologies, though village was totally detached from the nearby inhabitants. Their livelihoods mostly depended on the minor forest products and consumption of only raw vegetables, roots, fruits, nuts and minor millets. She reared buffaloes for milk purpose, in addition to sheep and poultry for meat purpose.

Further, she explained that the introduction of an NGO called Centre for Soil Salinity Research (CSSR) during 1996-97 and consequent meeting in their village on Environment and Pollution Free Life was the stepping stone for their village which motivated them towards modern civilisation. Among the tribal people, Valliammal showed interest towards the developmental activities. She voluntarily approached the officials of the NGO and collected information in connection with their empowerment. She was selected as the leader of that tribal village by the officials, because of her leadership quality and spontaneous active participation in all the meetings, demonstrations, etc.

She told that the first meeting of the NGO was about various scientific themes on how to be free from diseases and pollution and 'how to keep the environment clean'.

During the year 1997-98, the village was adopted by another NGO called NERD (Non-Conventional Energy for Rural Development) which organised programmes such as training on self employment, income generating activities, cleanliness, how to be courageous enough to face problems, power of decision making, etc. She was imparted skills on tailoring, bag knitting, crop cultivation, etc. for the empowerment of tribal community.

She described the changes that had taken place among them after undergoing the training programmes. The income generating activities helped them to earn some amount which contributed considerably to raise their family income.

During the year 1998-99, the tribal community was identified by the TANWA officials. They arranged all kinds of meetings, demonstrations on scientific way of crop cultivation, and income generating activities. The officials of TANWA explained the ways and means for starting self employment. The tribal woman narrated that the meetings conducted by the TANWA were highly useful for undertaking new practices, improving her skill on modern technologies such as seed treatment with bio-fertilisers, Azospirillum, Rhizobium and Phosphobacteria. She explained that the TANWA officials paved way for group activity. It helped them a lot to develop good qualities *viz.*, socialising, adjustment with any social kind, to be generous, human relations development, right approach to the financial institutions and taking joint decision making behaviour. These qualities improved her society. The officials of TANWA also selected Valliammal as the leader of a group of 16 member because of her distinguished involvement in the developmental activities. Her progressive nature helped others to avail the basic facilities.

In continuation of this, she approached the Block Development Officer (BDO) of Thondamuthur block and explained the situations existing in their households. She had a chance to meet the District Collector of Coimbatore with the support of the block development officials about the procedures to be followed to avail the facilities. Even though she was trained properly, she could not avail those facilities because of her ignorance. The District Collector visited the village along with the development officials. The Collector encouraged the tribal community to be energetic in achieving all the basic attributes. He took steps for taking available basic facilities, such as high school, medical facilities, drinking water, sanitation, and constructed new cement walled tiled house replacing the mud with thatched roof and arranged for income earning activities such as tailoring and basket knitting. Besides these, with the help of extension officials of state agriculture department, she could understand the technological bases of organic farming, preparation of EFYM, *Panchakavya*, vermicom-post preparation, etc.

On the recommendation of district Collector, her group was sanctioned Rs.1,00,000/- to start self employment activities. Further, she was supplied one tractor with cultivator and trailer free of cost so as to improve their farming. The Government supplied two cows in order to abolish the bonded labour as per the "Bonded Labour Abolition Act, 1976". The milk was supplied to the nearby milk society by engaging the unemployed men of their society which also facilitated men to get employment opportunity.

To alleviate the hurdles in transport facilities of her village, she had decided to run Autorickshaw from Sadivayal to Kovai Kutralam (Tourism place). She discussed the same with the Collector of Coimbatore district and the society members to get the consent for it. In view of above efforts, an auto was sanctioned on subsidy basis. She was very prompt in repayment of the loan. She selected two girls from their community and trained them in autorickshaw driving. Now, two autorickshaws are being operated from Sadivayal to Kovai Kutralam charging Rs. 2 to 5 per head. As a result of entrepreneurship training, she had taken effort to set up a business on marketing of forest products [Gooseberry, soapnut, *kadukkai, tharbai* grass, *puchikai* and *jadhikai* (nutmeg)] and marketed them at Erode on cost basis.

Further more, she had shifted their cultivation method from paddy to marigold with Coleus as intercropping system due to water shortage. The heavy scented blooms were sent to a perfumery at Karamadai. She said that the advantage with marigold was the perfumeries accept even dried flowers. So, wastage was minimal. To save input cost, some flowers were left out on the shrub itself so that she need not spend money on seeds. Otherwise, she would have spent nearly Rs. 600/ha.

The foothills of the Boluvampatti range also boasts of a lush forest, home to a variety of sweet-smelling flora. The Khadi and Village Industries Commission (KVIC) had given 10 boxes with queen bees to tribal women free of cost. She had been given training on the same.

She utilised the opportunity provided by the developmental departments. She had taken maximum efforts to bring economic revolution in her society in addition to social awareness and self confidence. The extraordinary and sincere effort made by her was appreciated by the officials and she was appointed as the President of Marudham Tribal Women's Federation (MTWF). It was an association of 18 tribal women self help group (SHGs).

Apart from these, she was also interested in political activities. She said that, if opportunity arises, she would participate and do better services for her society.

The unique features of this case of tribal woman who gained success through out reach programmes are:

- Courage
- Self confidence
- Self responsibility
- Better educational quality
- Good leadership quality
- Best organiser of group activity
- Good planner
- Voluntary and active participation in the developmental activities
- High entrepreneurship quality
- Positive attitude towards empowerment of women.

Conclusion

It could be concluded from the above case analysis, that the achievements of the tribal women are due to the concerted effort taken by the developmental organisations. The aforesaid are the evidences for her empowerment identified from the case analysis.

Thus, the results of the case analysis gives tangible evidence for the various empowerment dimensions such as extension, social, economic, scientific, psychologic and political dimensions. Ultimately, these empowerment dimensions contributed towards the high to very high level of empowerment.

References

1. Shylashri, C. (2001). **Socio – Economic Aspects of Women's Education – A Case Study of Bangalore,** Unpub.Ph.D, Thesis, Dept of Economics, UAS, Bangalore.
2. Seekabeer, N., (2004). **Women's Empowerment in the Context of Human Security,** 7-8, December, ESCAP, Bangok, Thailand.
3. Shobha Raghuram, (2003). **The Position and Condition of Women in India: Challenging the Darkness, Restoring faiths.** NSS manual on Women's development and Gender justice, Banglore, India, PP 62-66.
4. Swaminathan, M.S., (2003). **Creating the Instruments for a knowledge Revolution in Rural India.** MSSRF, The Hindu dt: 20 July, 2003.
5. Vasanthi Devi., (2004). **Women Study.** The Hindu dt: 11 March, 2004.
6. Vijayalakshmi Pandit, (1997). **Empowerment of women through Distance Education.** Book links corporation, Hyderabad.

Chapter 16

Reaching Out to the Youth : Methodology of Jan Sikshan Sansthan

V. Balasubramaniyan

Introduction

India which has opened up its economy, needs to invest in skill development, education and training of the workforce, so as to ensure their meaningful existence in the society. Every year, 5.5 million students pass out from class X of which 3.3 million go to class XI, leaving 2.2 million out of the education system. There are also dropouts after Class VIII, numbering 19 million. These are the children who look for vocational education and training and self employment avenues. Therefore, vocational education and training has a target group of 21 million, which is many times the number going into the institutes of higher learning and universities. Against this, the available formal training capacity of the country is only 2.3 million students which leaves a gap of 18.7 million.

The present work seeks to examine the experiments conducted at Avinashilingam Jan Shikshan Sansthan, Coimbatore since 1984, mobilising the community resources, infrastructure, expertise, and manpower, extensively for training and employment generation to the above said target groups including illiterates.

Institute of People's Education (IPE)

The Jan Shikshan Sansthan (formerly known as Shramik Vidyapeeth) is an innovative educational scheme in the field of non-formal and continuing education and training for adults, started by the Government of India in the year

1967, when the first Shramik Vidyapeeth was set up at Mumbai (Worli). The distinct features of the Sansthan are:

(i) flexibility characteristics of non-formal education,

(ii) the special target group of the socially, economically and educationally deprived sections of the society and

(iii) the objectives of offering life enrichment education (multi-faceted education) that is meant to provide the individual not only the skills to enhance his/her productive potentials but also the knowledge necessary for him/her to improve the quality of life through Life Enrichment Education (LEE) programmes.

The activities of the Jan Shikshan Sansthan (JSS) include: organising vocational courses (skill formation as well as skill up-gradation), awareness/life enrichment education programmes, income generating programmes, literacy, post-literacy and continuing education related programmes and establishing linkages with different developmental agencies and other organisations.

UNESCO was interested in promoting this type of education in India. The scheme promotes the utilisation of community resources for training and development. Yugoslavia had achieved success in the experiment of such scheme. The first Jan Shikshan Sansthan was established in Mumbai in March 1967. Encouraged by the successful functioning of this Jan Shikshan Sansthan, Government of India gradually expanded the scheme to other parts of the country. The period 1981-1986 was marked by a rapid expansion of the Jan Shikshan Sansthans in the country. As many as 28 Jan Shikshan Sansthans were started in the first six year period. During this period, Avinashilingam Jan Shikshan Sansthan was established in Coimbatore, on 2nd October 1984 under the auspices of Sri Avinashilingam Educational Trust Institutions, a pioneer - Deemed

University in Home Science education, having rich experience in developmental work for the urban and rural poor. Later, the Jan Shikshan Sansthans increased in number step-by-step, covering the whole country.

Avinashilingam Jan Shikshan Sansthan has been envisaged to be an institution of education to the poor. Its primary responsibility is to explore, innovate, work out alternatives, try new methodologies and thus meet the needs of different groups. This scheme envisages the utilisation of community resources rather than creating and establishing infrastructural facilities for the purpose of training and development.

Collaboration - Economy of Sharing

Avinashilingam Jan Shikshan Sansthan has an inbuilt system of collaborating with many organisations, institutions and agencies, and designs the programmes flexibly to suit the needs of the collaborators and target groups by which the scheme has far reaching results. The workplace is an excellent site for learning.

Excellent rapport has been developed by Avinashilingam Jan Shikshan Sansthan with collaborators of various kinds in Coimbatore, such as industries, motor vehicles service stations, hospitals, educational and technical institutions, printing press, etc. More than 700 organisations of these kinds are providing practical training to the youth. Collaboration in general is sought to achieve the objective of the JSS, *viz,* offering practical training and life enrichment education. The very strength of this JSS is its collaborators. Thus, collaboration plays a vital role in the conduct of training programmes.

The beneficiaries of JSS on becoming successful entrepreneurs, collaborate with JSS directly and help to impart on the job practical skill training to the beneficiaries of JSS.

Target Groups

The target groups for JSS include the socio-economically backward and educationally disadvantaged groups of urban/rural population such as men, women and youth, employed, self -employed, neo-literates, prospective workers and their family members as well as unemployed youth. Priority is to be given to adult neo-literates/semi-literates, SC and ST, women/girls, oppressed, migrants, slum/pavement dwellers and working children.

Hospitals/Clinical Laboratories

The trainees in Intensive Critical Care Unit Nursing Assistant course are placed for practical training in hospitals where there are greater ICCU facilities. The Operation Theatre Nursing Assistant trainees are sent to the hospitals where there are greater theatre facilities. Those trainees undergoing training in Ophthalmic Nursing Assistants are placed for practical training in various eye hospitals only. The trainees who have chosen Laboratory technician course for their study are sent to different laboratories for practical training. Thus, the trainees are exposed to various aspects of the hospital.

Industries/Workshops

Industries collaborate with Avinashilingam Jan Shikshan Sansthan to impart training for both men and women. Industrial electronics and power electronics, Turner, Fitter, Machinist, Welding training are imparted. Stipend is paid to the trainees in turner, fitter, machinist and welding courses. These courses are of six months duration. The stipend paid is Rs. 700 during the period of training. Computer Numerical control (CNC) Lathe operators course is also conducted with a stipend of Rs. 700 for the first three months and Rs. 800 for the next three months respectively.

Tool and dye making course is an industry-based course conducted in this JSS for one year. These trainees are sent for practical to industries and a stipend amount of Rs. 700 for fist six months and Rs. 800 for the second six months is being paid to them. There is great demand for these trainees both in the country and abroad.

Service Stations

The trainees of Two wheeler motor vehicles repairing, Four wheeler motor vehicles repairing, Auto Electrician, Refrigeration and Air conditioner repairing trades are sent for practical training to the service stations/workshops. More than 200 service stations/workshops are collaborating with JSS for the conduct of training.

Courses Offered

The courses offered are varied in nature and are based on the manpower requirement of various industries and organisations in Coimbatore. All the courses are need-based, tailor-made and non-formal to suit the target groups. Avinashilingam Jan Shikshan Sansthan is offering more than 115 types of training programmes for employment, self employment and entrepreneurship development. These include: Turner, Fitter, Welder, Machinist, Tool and Die making, Computer Numerical Control (CNC) Lathe Operator, Electrician, Motor winding, Refrigerator and Air conditioners repairing, Radio and Television repairing, cell phone repairing, plumbing, two wheeler motor vehicles repairing, four wheeler motor vehicles repairing, auto electrician, operation theatre assistant, intensive critical care unit assistant, dental nursing assistant, orthopaedic nursing assistant, ophthalmic technician, maternity and child health, occupational therapy nursing assistant, gift articles making, soft toys making, variety of paintings, beauty culture, etc.

Bakery, soft toys making, jam and juice making, soup and snacks preparation, artificial flower making, gift articles making, pot painting, hair cutting, mehandhi application, glass painting, fabric painting, metal embossing, metal engraving, nib painting, mural pearl painting, sand drawing, tiles painting, etc. are some of the other very short duration vocational training programmes.

The selected boys and girls, men and women of various courses are placed with collaborators for 6 to 8 hours a day to work on the job and learn practical skills. This sort of practical training is very useful to the learners as it is being given in the actual field situation instead of a model laboratory established for this purpose.

Theory and life enrichment education are given in Avinashilingam Jan Shikshan Sansthan and its extension centers located in industries, slums, and rural areas for 1 ½ hours to 2 hours a day.

Advantages of Vocational Training Programmes

- It teaches the trainees job-readiness skills.
- It helps to learn skills that the employers value.
- During the work-based learning experiences, it provides an exposure to a professional environment and to work well with other people.
- Jobs that a candidate obtains through vocational training, tends to be different from and of higher quality than the jobs normally got.
- The beneficiaries of need-based training have better labour market outcome.
- No investment to the Institution.
- Short duration training.
- Employment is assured to the beneficiaries.
- On the job experiences create potential for effective leadership development.

A. Individuals are placed in a variety of challenging situations with problems to solve and choices to make under conditions of risk. Such situations (i) motivate individuals to learn (ii) provide opportunities to gain new ideas and knowledge and to practice skills and apply knowledge and it also (iii) encourages new insights through reflections on prior actions.

B Individuals gain their experiences in a supportive environment with the supervisors who act as positive role models and give constructive support and become mentors to provide counsel.

Resource Persons

Resource persons include training faculty. The Avinashilngam Jan Shikshan Sansthan has no core faculty. Coimbatore being a good educational and business centre, availability of required guest faculty is easy. They are selected / invited through personal contacts of the Director and suggestions of the board members, advisory committee.

Resource persons are competent, qualified and have experience in their specific area of teaching. They have a feeling of pride to get involved in a social cause by teaching at JSS. Competent and qualified persons in a wide array of fields with years of experience, working in various organisations and educational institutions such as Industrial Training Institutes, Polytechnic colleges, Sri Avinashilingam Institute for Home Science and Higher Education for Women, Banks, District Industries Center, Tamil Nadu Industrial Investment Corporation, Small Industries Service Institute, Small Industries Development Bank of India, Bharathiar University, Sri Ramakrishna Mission Vidyalaya and professionals like lawyers, doctors, engineers, retired army officers, sales tax practitioners, etc are involved as resource persons.

Life Enrichment Education (LEE)

Value oriented education, discipline and character building are the major social benefits for an all round development of the learners. Life Enrichment Education includes Personality Development, Communication Skills, Interpersonal Relationship, Work Culture, Work Ethics, Self-development, Self-confidence Building, Knowledge about their day-to-day living, Health Education, Nutrition Education, Population Education, Aids Awareness, Home Nursing, Home Management, Time Management, Preservation of Environment, Art of Living, etc.

LEE is conducted with the help of excellent team of resource persons. They are specially trained and experienced in various fields.

Monitoring

The performance of the learners, on the job, in practical training is being monitored everyday. The learners will maintain diaries, writing their time of arrival, time of departure, learning on the job everyday in industries and other agencies, which will be checked by the works / duty in-charge in the shop floor and the teacher in the class. This kind of monitoring system ensures regularity, involvement, discipline and learning outcome of the participants. Further to this, the learners will wear uniform, on the job and hold identity card.

Placement

The learners get employment immediately after the training. The success behind the employment assurance is the result of the collaboration by the institution with Industries and other organisations; starting from manpower assessment, to on the job training, good rapport with the collaborators and follow up.

Continuing Education

The learners, such as illiterates and school dropouts are given opportunity in literacy education and continuing education to obtain academic qualification.

Entrepreneurship Training

The learners get employment immediately after the training. The institution promotes self-employment and entrepreneurship activity to the ex-learners after a two to three year period, by giving more opportunity and practice on the job, EDP training and guidance to start their own enterprise.

Follow Up Post-evaluation meetings and Self-Employment

A follow up is maintained to assess the benefits accrued by the trainees collecting information about their employment or income generating status, either through self-employment, wage employment, or co-employment. Letters/information/feed back received from the trainees are documented from time to time. Entrepreneurship and employment guidance is also provided to the trainees.

Various service stations, hospitals and industries also approach the JSS for manpower requirement. Since the JSS beneficiaries are of character and efficiency, the demand for such manpower has increased by leaps and bounds.

Success Stories

Innumerable number of trainees have succeeded in life, mainly because of the skill training underwent at Avinashilingam Jan Shikshan Sansthan. Few important cases have been presented here. Important opinions and valuable suggestions made by them are listed at the end. Poverty, physical handicap, deserted by family, and inadequate school education etc did not prevent the trainees from succeeding in life.

Mrs.Bagyalakshmi
Two-Wheeler Mechanic

Separated from her husband, Bagyalakshmi felt deserted. Hailing from the Goldsmith family, due to poverty, many of her relatives committed suicide. Bagya's husband deserted her because of insufficient income. Something from inside was telling her that she could choose some profession, which is equally good to men folk. She underwent two-wheeler training and is now a trustworthy employee with a Honda Dealer. Now she can drive a scooter. She is trained to do things differently and learn the concepts in a systematic way. Being independent and earning Rs. 1,500 per month, she claims that she can be a role model to other women who are helpless.

Born and brought up in a remote village near Theni, with a polio-affected leg, Jayachithra entered AJSS during her visit to her relatives place. The day enlightened her to visualize her future, as she thought her family with 5 girls and one young boy would be helped. Now, only 26, she is able to steer her family. She arranged for the marriage of her two elder sisters. An unemployed B.Com student, she joined AJSS Beautician Course and now a post-graduate in Commerce, owns a tailoring unit with a Beauty Parlour. The monthly income of Rs. 10,000 enabled her to save around Rs. 3 lakh and plan to go for a house in another one year.

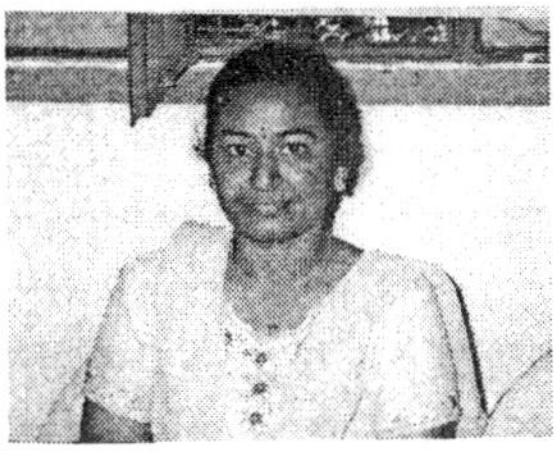

Jayachithra
Beautician and Tailoring

Graduation in English Literature did not fetch him any job or even he could not have any idea about his future. The R & A.C course with AJSS has totally changed his life. Now an Authorised dealer of Voltas Air conditioners, he employs more than 20 people with a monthly salary ranging from Rs. 3, 000 to Rs. 4, 000. He employs only the trainees of AJSS that really made him succeed in business. The commitment, involvement, real enthusiasm in executing the job and the skill base are remarkable talents of AJSS trainees. The virgin field chosen by Manoj has helped him survive and enrich his life in all fronts. With his monthly income of about Rs. 75,000 he invested Rs. 20 Lakhs and saved about Rs. 6 lakhs.

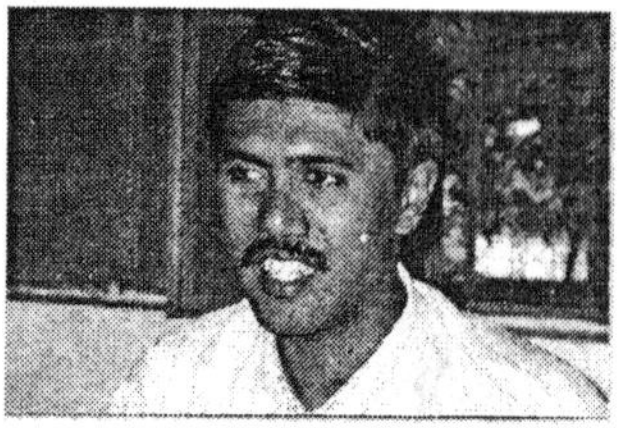

Manoj Kumar
Refrigeration & A.C. Mechanic

Born deaf and dumb with physical deformities, with no family support, Saravanan was adopted by the NGO "Families for Children". He is not only the breadwinner for self, but also contributes some money to his parents. His monthly income runs around Rs. 5,000 And his contribution to his parents is Rs. 1,500. The painting and Greeting Cards making skills learnt from AJSS helped him achieve this. He has to his credit many awards at the local, national and international for the best drawing. He got orders from the UNICEF for the supply of greeting cards. The cheerful face itself will reveal the joy of his life, which made him forget the physical inability.

Saravanan
Painter

Proud mother of two sons, and one daughter, all being Engineers, struggled a lot to succeed in life. Though employed in a senior position, due to loss in the factory, her husband could not fetch any money for the survival of the family. With HSC discontinued, she joined soft toy making training with AJSS. She was raw in converting herself as an entrepreneur. She underwent the Women Entrepreneur Development Programme at AJSS, and she was able to set up a soft toy making unit. After meeting out all expenses, she is able to make good Rs. 7,500 per month as profit. She directly employed 5 persons and given job orders to more than 20 persons and made each one of them to earn more than Rs. 7,000 per month. She is supporting her family and acquired wealth worth about Rs. 6 lakh within a period of 4 years. Her approach towards the customer, public relations skills and mainly the habit as a family manager has shown significant improvement.

Susheela
Soft Toys Making

It is hard to remove the smile from her face. Deaf and dumb, with an education of 8th standard, she was neglected, not allowed to do anything on her own. AJSS is capable enough to train a girl of such a calibre, Embroidery, Fabric painting and Oil painting. The training and the atmosphere at AJSS made her speak, and learn Bharatanatyam. She continued to learn many other skills in painting. She singly can travel to the neighbouring town Tiruppur, 40 Kms away from Coimbatore and sell her paintings to known persons. She makes around Rs. 1,500 per month. She tells, "I do not know how I learnt speaking, since I am deaf. I study the face and movement of the lips of the persons talking to me. The friendly atmosphere created by the trainees and the teachers at AJSS helped me to overcome my handicap. I found the real meaning of my life."

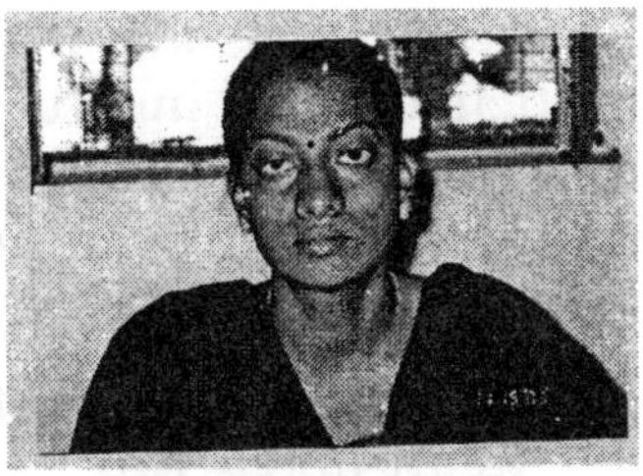

Tharageswari
Painting

Shaping the Future

In order to achieve social harmony and peace along with economic development, the dropouts from school and university system should be given an opportunity to shape their future by acquiring skills.

Vocational education and training is required for a large number of people covering various socio-economic sectors, and covering local occupations as well as those where global competition is required. New approaches to vocational education and training and development aimed at global competitiveness could be successful only through purposeful collaboration between trainers, trainees, employers, employees and the community. Vocational courses should be demand and need-based, keeping in mind the constantly changing requirements of technologies/ industries. This requires identification of future needs of industries with respect to skills, keeping in view the changes in technology and industry.

The Second Labour Commission has recommended participation of institution, Government, industry and trade sector to provide training for the work force through a modular approach in vocational training.

Vocational education and training in India needs fresh outlook and the following suggestions may be useful to make full use of resources and the youth energies for the national development:

- Prepare the youth for a vocation of their choice.
- Build up a formidable work force of an international quality which would have demand not only in India but also in all other countries.
- Development of a world class skilled man power in the manufacturing service sector.
- Trained personnel in agriculture especially in floriculture, horticulture, sericulture and fishery are

needed for diversification of agriculture and increasing export of agricultural products.

- India must become an international hub for manufacturing, trading and services.
- The duration of vocational courses should be carefully assessed so as to provide flexibility and vertical mobility.
- The vocational courses should be demand and need based, keeping in mind the constantly changing requirement of technologies/industries. This requires identification of future needs of industries with respect to skills, keeping in view the changes in technology and industry.

The forecasting of future skills should be done at national level for a period of five years and the vocational courses should have in-built flexibility to allow students to switch courses with changes in demand pattern.

This is virtually an alternative system of education. As an alternative system of education, vocational training for those dropouts who need appropriate skills essential for gainful employment, deals with a flexible course curriculum and teaching methodology with cost effective educational infrastructure.

The International Commission for Education for the twenty first century under the Chairmanship Jacques Dellors, has pointed out that education throughout the life of an individual is based on four pillars - Learning to know, Learning to do, Learning to live together and Learning to be.

Chapter 17

Dimensions of Community Outreach Methodologies - Rajagiri Experience

Binoy Joseph and M.P. Antoni

Introduction

Rajagiri College of social sciences is one of the pioneering institutions in south India in the area of training in human service profession. The college, started in 1955 as the department of social work at Sacred Heart College, Thevara has grown in such a way that it has two campuses having a variety of courses ranging from BSW to MBA and Engineering. What makes it different from other social work institutes is its immense focus on the element of community outreach programmes along with its classroom focused theoretical training for the social work trainees. By giving a focused notice to the child and elder -centered intervention of Rajagiri, this paper concentrates on the persistent and unwavering efforts of Rajagiri college to start and sustain a variety of extension/outreach programmes The different programmes have got their own methodologies and delivery mechanisms for ensuring people's participation.

Our Experience

Social work education is not to be seen as a process of classroom exercise, but as a way of being close to people, catering to their needs and solving their problems. The fact that learning social work is not acquiring a University Degree, but being open to varied experiences through experiments, reflections, sharing and action should he emphasised. For this, Schools of Social Work should be able to develop community outreach departments operating as satellite units in different parts of the society. Now we experience in the campus our students going to people, being with them, learning with them. They are enthused to reach out to the community's needs. We see a number of social work students coming from International Universities. There are a number of neighbourhood communities empowered at the community level; our college is in touch with a number of organisations at the grassroot level, Government and Non-Government level. Our teachers are not merely givers of knowledge, but also practitioners. Observing its Golden Jubilee this year, Rajagiri College, throughout its history of more than five decades, has been striving to be a model school of social work education through the process of continuous exploration, experimentation and incorporation of new areas in the field of research, consultancy, training and practice. Rooted at Rajagiri Campus, the college has been able to extend its services to different parts of the state.

Intervention through *Kudumbashree*

Rajagiri has also stepped up to join hands with *Kudumbashree* in the exertion of social development through poverty eradication. An agreement has been signed between *Kudumbashree* and Rajagiri College to place MSW/ BSW students with the different *Panchayats* in Ernakulam District to work as Voluntary Executives. Before the students are sent to the *Panchayats,* they are given a three-day intensive and well-structured training at Rajagiri by Resource Persons from Kudumbashree Mission Office. At present, in more than 50 *Panchayats,* students are offering their services which range from helping members of Neighbourhood (NHG), ADS (Area Development Society) and CDS (Community Development Society) in dealing with accounts, reports, meetings and micro-enterprises to helping in the preparation of yearly plan documents for the *Panchayats.*

It was proved that the results were significant. The arrival of a formally trained social worker made a big impact on the way *Kudumbashree* programmes were being planned and implemented. From handling family counseling to increasing the spread of lease land farming, the young social workers have made their presence felt. Students have been able to go beyond the targets set. They have been able to improve thrift collection, increase the spread of lease land farming, create better awareness about AIDS, alcoholism and arrange for classes for Ashraya Project (A programme to launch focused rehabilitation of identified destitute in each *Panchayat*), home management and simple accounting methods.

Live Labs

Rajagiri college of social sciences has the vision of becoming not only a centre of excellence in the field of social work education and promoting a holistic form of learning but also integrating social commitment and concern of social sciences, promoting the concept of Live Labs. The Live Labs are programmes in which students, faculty, and social work practitioners work together to serve the community by encouraging student intervention and participation. The coinage of the term 'Live Labs' for different extension departments under the college has got the basis and meaning of serving its underlining principle to provide practice-training opportunities just like laboratory for the human service trainees. One of the major thrusts behind initiating such Live Labs right inside the campus has been the prospect for providing focused attention to the students during their practice training within the campus apart from sending them to outside agencies for placements. The extension departments (re-christened as Live Labs) initiated from the 70's include the following:

- NSS Training and Orientation Centre, Kerala (NSS-TOC)

- Middle Level Training Center (MLTC)
- Rajagiri Research Institute
- Community Aid and Sponsorship Programme (CASP)
- Anganwadi Ttraining Centre (AWTC)
- Voluntary Coordinating Agency for Adoption (VCA)
- CHILDLINE
- Rajagiri Family Counseling Centre (RFCC) and
- Rajagiri Outreach Service Society.

The recent intervention of Rajagiri at the time of the catastrophe of tsunami, the rehabilitation efforts of Rajagiri Live Labs at the time of need has won tremendous appreciation from different corners of society. It can be cited as an example for the spirit of social commitment. As a step towards achieving Rajagiri's vision of community development through community participation, these Live Labs act as change agents or facilitators to ensure progress in a variety of interventions initiated by Rajagiri or in partner organisations.

Child-centered Interventions

With the conviction that through a child, a family and through a family, a community as a whole can be empowered, Rajagiri as its major intervention strategy, developed Live Labs that would help in dealing with various issues related to children. In this regard, protecting child rights and providing opportunity for education and growth through CASP, providing a support and future to abandoned children through VCA for adoption and Indian Council of Social Welfare (ICSW), reaching out to children in distress situation through CHILDLINE, providing counseling and guidance through Rajagiri Family Counseling Centre are a few of our initiatives taken up in addressing the needs and problems of children. By initiating a Child Rights Resource Centre (CRRC), Tots Care and the Chapter of Campaign Against Child Labour (CACL) in

Kerala, the College continues its efforts to protect the rights of every child in our society at large. Rajagiri has built partnership in coordination with these agencies to see that various dimensions of child rights like right to survival, right to protection, right to development and the right to participation are addressed and initiatives are taken by the community members themselves.

The CASP in Focus

Organised in 1975 as a national level NGO in Pune, Community Aid and Sponsorship Programme is a child centered project, extending to the community to meet it basic needs. With the vision of upholding the rights and dignity of every individual especially the children, CASP

- enables children, their families and communities to meet their basic needs.
- enhances their ability to participate in and benefit from their social environment, and
- promotes the rights and interests of the child.

As a collaborative venture, Rajagiri College of Social Sciences and CASP tied up to start a new project namely CASP-Rajagiri Sponsorship Project in 1982, with the objective of upgrading the quality and volume of the services provided, by taking advantage of the valuable skills and resources of leading social work institution. So far, CASP-Rajagiri could significantly improve the quality of life of over 2050 children through sponsorship and related activities. The basic function of CASP-Rajagiri project is to help the underprivileged children to start or continue their education and strengthen their social and psychological environment. Its assistance caters to the following categories of children:

- Children whose families are in crisis.
- Differently abled children.
- Mentally handicapped.

- Children of Leprosy/HIV/AIDS parents.
- Children of imprisoned parents.

A support system is working for the sponsored children and their families, in each of the communities, guided and facilitated by professional social workers. This ensures that the children sponsored through CASP receive opportunities for an integrated growth rather than an academic-oriented facilitation. The support system goes in line with sponsorship aid so that an ideal blending of curricular as well as extra-curricular orientation is offered to the children.

Services for Senior Citizens

The fast growing number of elderly population in the world is a challenge before the human society considering its impact on the individuals, family, community and society at large due to various reasons, thanks to the advanced medical technologies, which helped people having increased life expectancy with less mortality and high morbidity. What comes to the picture about the elderly population, is not only of the destitute, but that a large portion of the economically and physically fit senior citizens require social security, emotional and psychological support and community support for the wholesome existence. It is anticipated that only a familial support network and a strong social security system can remedy the situation. Non-institutional care system/programme like Day Care Centres would be an answer provided it is properly administered. The day care centre at Kothad Island by CASP-Rajagiri Sponsorship Project of Rajagiri College is one such model, which can be adapted with necessary modifications to local situation.

Rajagiri College of Social Sciences, through its Live Lab of CASP, started its, intervention in the island in the year 1991. Several projects and programmes with people's initiative have been taken up there over the years. The day care centre was the result of such an experiment. The centre commenced its functioning on the 15th of March, 1977 and continues its services/activities on two full days in a week i.e.Tuesdays and Fridays without any break. The centre serves as a medium for free expression of the problems and frustration of the elders in the community. It acts as a centre for recreation, cultural exchange, medical attention, etc.

A day starts at the centre with the inter-religious prayer session followed by *yoga* (exercises). Then the inmates sit together to analyse local new read out by the volunteer. And together, they prepare lunch and enjoy the noon meal. In between they interact and involve in playing games, sessions on relevant subjects, cultural presentations by members, indoor games, celebrations of birthdays of the members and important days and watching T.V./VCD entertainments.

People from different family background come here. Their behaviour is also different. But being together is something special. None at the centre has difference of opinion and feeling about its utility. Considering its triumph, Rajagiri has successfully tried the same experiment with communities such as Kalamassery, Manappuram, Puthusserymala in the districts of Ernakulam and Alleppy.

Community Development

Rajagiri is the pioneer in initiating the concept of partnership in community development. On the lines of various Govt. initiatives like-people's planning programme, Kerala Development Project, etc. we also ensured community partnership in development through formation of NHG's, CDS, etc. to implement various programmes addressing the specific needs of the community like drinking water, sanitation, housing, etc. This also ensured sustainability of the programme. We also used to facilitate the projects of corporate establishments like Cochin Refineries Ltd., on one side and on the other, we raised resources locally and internationally for social development. Our efforts in Kalamassery Municipality through Rajagiri Community Development Scheme, Asia's No.1 Solar electrification and drinking water project at Mundanmudi, Total sanitation project at Kothad, Model village scheme at Alacode Panchayat sponsored by HUDCO, Rotary Kadamakudy Development Project at Kadamakudy, etc. are some of the significant experiments in the field of community development.

Women Empowerment

Rajagiri recognises the importance of addressing the problems related to women and instituted the Centre For Women Studies and Development. The centre gathers and updates the new thoughts and philosophies on women's empowerment. Rajagiri works with various State and National bodies like National Women's Commission, State Women's Commission, Central Social Welfare Board, Rashtriya Mahila Kosh to achieve women empowerment in its true sense.

Other programmes initiated are promotion of SHGs by encouraging women to become self-reliant and economically independent. As we discussed already, we also work in association with *Kudumbashree* projects of Govt. of Kerala to strengthen the cause of women empowerment. Gender sensitisation programmes are relentlessly conducted in all communities where we have interventions to propagate the concept of equality among men and women.

Environment

Rajagiri has always striven to be an example to other campuses in building environment friendly attitudes and practices. Our campus is declared as Litter-free and Zero Waste Management and we promote the concept of clean and eco-friendly campuses. These small initiatives have had a large impact on the Rajagiri Community that include faculty, staff, students and an extended impact on the families and communities from where we come. Our various steps in conserving nature's precious resources include using and promoting non-conventional energy sources through Aditya Solar Shop, Rain Water harvesting units, Bio-gas Plants, Plantation of trees under the scheme, Haritabiyanam, etc.

Health

Rajagiri has been involved in promoting health and taking up health issues ever since 1980's. The initiatives were begun by stationing the offices of Kerala Voluntary Health Services, the state unit of Voluntary Health Association of India (VHAI). Later on, many innovative programmes were initiated by Rajagiri such as Child-to-child Health programme, School Health Programme, *Arogya Mela*, etc.

We also have taken steps in promoting usage of indigenous medicines, Ayurveda etc. through conducting Distance Education Programmes, medical camps, etc. by both students and Live Labs in various communities.

Reformative Activities

Rajagiri has always been in the forefront of many social reforms and we have initiated the process of an integration of legal system and social work practices. As a first step Rajagiri Legal Aid Cell was formulated, whereby free legal assistance is provided to the community members. Legal aid clinics, legal awareness camps and seminars, service in family courts and *Lok Adalats*, Sponsorship assistance to children of prisoners etc. are the other related steps through which the institution has provided a role for the social workers in the legal arena.

Education and Peace

Rajagiri's vision of education encompasses all round formation, community of committed teachers, family-centered education, making education available to all aspiring students and above all a just and human society as ultimate goal. Keeping the dictum "Think Globally, act Locally" in mind, Rajagiri has developed an educational system, whereby interaction and global exchange was made possible for students and Universities from other Countries & States, through Rajagiri International Exchange Programme (RIEP). LIVE LABS like NSS-TOC, AWTC, MLTC, Research Institute etc. Moral School Camps and Career Guidance Camps for the children of the State during vacation make our efforts more meaningful and future oriented.

Conclusion

Rajagiri strides forward to future carrying the good messages from the experiences of the past. The college believes that it has done its finest to provide opportunities for Social Work Practitioners and Trainees to intervene in almost every sphere. Really, this has increased the compass of professional social work in Kerala. Being a pioneer social work Institute in Kerala, we also stand out as the role model for various NGOs and Social Work Institutes to promote social work practice in a systematic, scientific and methodical manner.

References

1. George Joseph & P.O.George edited Social Work Education-Emerging Concerns Rajagiri College of Social Sciences, Rajagiri.
2. Handbook of Rajagiri College of Social Sciences, 2002.
3. "Students as agents of social change," The Hindu, Friday, December 31, 2004.

Chapter 18

Reaching out to the Community of Small Rubber Growers

Usha Rani, S.

Role of Rubber Board

The Indian Rubber Board was constituted under the Rubber (Production and Marketing) Act of 1947.On amending this act, the Rubber Board came into existence on 1st of August, 1955. With a clear framework for the discharge of functions and mode of implementation, the ultimate aim of the Board has been the development of rubber plantation industry in India.

Initially introduced as a crop of the affluent farmers, gradually-within 15 years after formation of Rubber Board-rubber became a subsistence crop for small and marginal farmers of India, in the rubber growing tracts. Now, rubber plantation sector includes 86 per cent of small holdings, majority with an extent below four hectares, in the range of 0.2 ha. to four hectors.

Factors behind the success of the rubber were i) the unique features of the extension system and ii)the values nurtured or existed in the system. These two factors together had facilitated effective outreach.

This article is an attempt to analyse the outreach to the community by Rubber Board, which is the Governmental agency for the development of rubber plantation industry in India.

In India, around 30,000 different articles are produced out of rubber. At the global level, it forms the principal raw material in the manufacture of around 56,000 different articles ranging from feeding bottle nipples to gigantic earth moving truck tyres. The range of articles manufactured out of rubber and their influence in the day-to-day life made modern life greatly reliant on rubber. The dependence of modern life on this precious material is so massive which made civilised life on earth itself impossible without rubber.

Extension System of Rubber Board

The development and extension activities of Rubber Board are implemented through Rubber Production Department; headed by Rubber Production Commissioner. Totally, 39 Regional Offices, each headed by a Deputy Rubber Production Commissioner or Development Officer, situated in major rubber growing tracts of the country coordinate the activities in the field. Regional Offices are supported by Field stations and the activities under the Field stations are managed by the Field officers. The Field Officers to whom the grassroots level extension activities in the field are entrusted with, are graduates in Agriculture or post graduates in Botany. They function like the eyes and ears of the Rubber Board.. The main characteristic of the system is that the development and extension activities are integrated and decentralised. Effective two-way information flow is facilitated enabling the diffusion of updated farm science to the community with feedback on problems from the farm to find apt solutions.

Organisational Features

Organisationally, a commodity based Extension system, with R&D linkage, had been operative in Rubber Board. Transfer of Technology to narrow down the gap between the lab and the land was the focus of outreach. The system had been designed to function based on the diffusion model. As explained by B.E. Swanson & J.B.Clear (1984), the model assumed a shift from traditional methods of production to new, science-based methods of production that include new technological components such as new varieties, cultural practices....' In the case of rubber, several peculiar features were noticeable in the extension system.

Community participation: The salient organisational feature of the Rubber Board's extension system was that the community to be reached were not left out of policy making. Constitutionally, the Board members include representatives of the small growers, large growers and even estate workers. The participation of the representatives of the beneficiaries in the policy making body, was supportive in formulating schemes on feeling the pulse of the community. Such an approach offered a need-based orientation to the schemes and programmes.

Effective extension management: The system incorporated in it the elements of effective extension management including timely planning, implementation and evaluation of the outreach programmes. The activities in the field were coordinated, monitored and evaluated at fixed intervals. Solutions and suggestions for improvement were sought by the extension personnel. There were regular and constant interactions between the Extension Officers at different levels of management to ensure information flow and proper execution and monitoring.

Human resource development: The proficiency of the extension officials are updated through training imparted at the time of recruitment, as well as periodically. In addition to the theoretical part, there had been provisions for training in the field itself before entering the field work and as refresher programmes on updated technologies, which gave them the required skill and proficiency in their task.

Constant interaction and feedback: Constant interactions with the farmers in the field through group meetings, discussions, demonstrations and seminars had been another effective means of outreach. In addition, the conducting of annual promotional campaign facilitates the interaction with around one lakh growers effectively with a new message, each year. The annual promotional campaign also provides an opportunity for a thorough evaluation of a single concept or technology, and effective feedback.

Facilitation for planned change: Board's outreach programmes were not isolated efforts towards a solitary goal. But, a well planned change, with full packages of assistance to the growers meeting the requirements related to finance, inputs, technology and skill. The approach and methods had always facilitated to meet these requirements.

Approaches, methods and tools: Transfer of Technology through interpersonal mode was the initial approach for outreach, which soon encompassed group approach as well. The tools for outreach mainly include:

a) Interpersonal contacts including Advisory visits to impart advice on farm operations covering all aspects right from selection of land for cultivation, preliminary planting operations, planting, manuring, disease management, crop harvesting and crop processing.

b) Visits to the plantations to provide financial and technical support through implementation of various schemes. The salient features of the Board's schemes had been

- need based orientation
- focus on popularisation of new technologies
- ability to meet the financial, technological and material requirements of small growers as self-contained packages of assistance for development of rubber plantation
- provision for beneficiary contribution to ensure utilisation of own resources. (This approach had enabled the resource poor beneficiaries to find part of their livelihood as wages, through work while developing

their plantations in areas like North- Eastern states and in tribal plantation projects. This sowed the seed of success of development of rubber culture followed by expansion in a massive scale in the non-traditional areas, totally unfamiliar with rubber cultivation.)

- Setting up of trial/demonstration plots to witness the change, leading to popularisation of different technologies.
- Training and demonstrations in the field to enable the small growers to familiarise the technologies and develop skills to adopt the practices in their holdings.
- Conducting of seminars and group meetings facilitating extensive interaction within the community and the opportunities for dissemination of ideas.
- Conducting of promotional campaign, group meetings facilitating quick and wide dissemination of a specific theme within the community.
- Farmer Resource persons: Innovative technologies and scientific practices are popularised through successful farmers.
- Awards: Innovations and group attitudes were encouraged through awards for the best grower (Best Grower Award) and best group (Best RPS award).
- Use of print and visual media: Films and publication of periodicals, magazines and pamphlets were beneficial tools for popularising ideas, technologies and successful efforts, ensuring information flow and communication.
- Use of electronic media: Electronic media is also utilised for dissemination of ideas and two-way information flow. www.rubberboard.org.in is the official website of Rubber Board.
- Exposure visits for farmers: Impact of exposure visits like *'Sastradarsan'* programmes arranged under the idea of 'seeing and believing' was remarkable in bringing

about changes in a revolutionary manner in the non-traditional areas, particularly among the tribal people who traditionally believed in and practiced *'Jhumming'* (shifting cultivation) and to whom rubber was not only new but totally unheard of too.

- Promotion of group approach: Mobilising the community for collective action to address their own problems had been part of Board's outreach. Initially, Rubber Marketing Cooperatives, and later, Rubber Producers' Societies, and Rubber Swasraya Sangham (Rubber Self Help Groups) are being promoted. Institutional support is provided to strengthen their activities related to transfer of technology, service, human resource development, processing and marketing and ancillary income generation and to develop infrastructure.
- Market-led Extension: Market support is provided to the community based organisation through vertical integration with the companies, jointly promoted by the community based groups, the RPS, and Rubber Board. This alliance has been facilitating effective outreach, strengthening the community through opportunities for diversified market channels for their crop.

Reorientation of Outreach Strategies

Initially, the extension system was a miniature set up, operating with a small group of Extension Officers, but so was the target group too. But subsequently, when the number of units reached around a million by 2003, the extension officer: grower ratio was still 1:3000. Initially, the focus of outreach was Transfer of Technology. However, markets and community assumed the focus in development after 1980s. There was a shift in priorities from a tree centred approach to man centred approach, thus community assuming a core position.

To overcome the limitations imposed by the increased number of holdings and to attain global competency in the small holding rubber sector, effective outreach was essential. With this aim, efforts were made by the Board to introduce a participatory extension management system. The formation of Rubber Producers' Societies with the idea of self help at the grassroots level, as agency to facilitate outreach, was the successful and unique effort done in the history of outreach. This was a revamping of Community Driven Development approach, which was initiated earlier through cooperatives, the real zeal envisaged soon disappeared. Totally, 2160 Rubber Producers Societies were registered as village level association of small holders.

More than 300 of them have now developed the infra structure for processing with the assistance of Rubber Board. They function as the agency for outreach, as a center for transfer of technology, and input delivery. In addition, they help to increase the livelihood capabilities of their members who are smallholders through collective processing and marketing of the crop, providing service for adoption of scientific cultivation practices, ancillary income raising activities, social welfare activities, employment generation for the vulnerable section of the community and so on. The outreach mechanism had thus shifted to an empowerment approach since late 1980s.

Successful Outreach Values

Introduction of an alien crop unknown to the community enjoying unique pre-planting, planting, maintenance, exploitation and processing techniques was the major challenge of the extension machinery. This included creating the atmosphere for the change process, preparing the social setting as well as the mind set of the farmers. Assessing situations, reducing the change obstacles, bringing about the behavioural change, introducing strategies - all have been part of the effort. (A.J. Sofranko, 1984).The various outreach methods had been effective in bringing about the change. The extension personnel had got the advantage of practical training in all the cultivation practices in the field, from germination of seeds to processing. Also, within the community, innovative farmers were already under the influence and attraction of the glory of the crop. As early adopters, their influence in the community was also capitalised by the resource group by setting up demonstration plots, arranging interactions in this plot, etc. So, the social incentives - desire of economic improvement was already there. This coupled with Board's outreach with modern technologies, developed or modified by the Rubber Research Institute of India, through the extension machinery brought in the change – the development which is unparalleled in any crop.

In any Outreach, there are two counterparts - the one who wants to reach and the other one who is to be reached. Analysis of the Board's efforts and achievement reveals that for an effective outreach, there are certain basic values which the first group has to possess and certain characters desirable within the group to be reached. Some of the values of the Extension personnel are discussed here.

Knowledge: Here, the literary meaning does not imply the actual content relevant to the situation. Knowledge implies all the wisdom, insight and knowhow the change agent required for the outreach to the community, in the particular situation. He or they should have the wisdom to define the purpose (why) of outreach (the mission – being the familiar term),how it could be achieved (how) and what is to be achieved (what). These aspects require a thorough knowledge about the situation (micro and macro levels), process and the content. The skill, the aptitude the technical know how and proficiency related to technologies, extension and markets are all varied forms of this 'knowledge'.

Cognition: Means the perception or knowing in the widest sense. It is the capacity within a person, which could be natural or nurtured. Frequent experiences of analytical attitude of situations and processes will help to have a cognitive behaviour. Cognition has been found to generate effortful thinking, thus influencing the process by which attitudinal change occurs. (Petty and Cacioppo-1986).

Empathy: Literary meaning of empathy is "power of entering into another's personality and imaginatively experiencing his experience." Not only empathetic to a person, but empathising with the idea and the situation is one of the required values. Empathy generates emotional involvement, which is the factor tempting individuals to have devotion and sincerity in the work, programme or efforts. Efficiency, service mentality and dedication are generated from emotional involvement of the extension personnel with their mission. This is the key factor which makes outreach quick and steady.

Reflexivity: This is the ability to react according to the situation. It is essential to have the capacity for visioning. Effective outreach is possible only with a proper vision, getting emotionally involved in the vision, developing and analysing it, periodically to perfect it according to social, economic, spatial and temporal contexts.

Endurance: Tolerance to positive or negative organisational, environmental, behavioural changes demands high level of patience. Outreach to distant remote villages, necessitates endurance in experiencing happiness in performing field work even under inconducive situations like rain, sun, cold and even at the risk of life while practicing in areas like North-east-in places of active revolutionary extremists.

The qualities of the outreach group will not alone involve miracles but there are some important characters of the group to be reached. We will analyse a few of them, which the author has experienced among the community of rubber growers.

Desire for change: There should be an intense longing for change in the community where the outreach is proposed. The felt need as we always denote it, should arise from the socio-economic conditions of life, or as explained by Maslow's theory on hierarchy of needs, it could be for some other aspirations such as physiological, security, affection, affiliation, esteem and self orientation. If the desire is not there, the change agent is bound to create it, applying his 'knowledge' in a context-specific manner.

Cooperation: Only if the community or the members of the community are cooperative to the efforts to initiate the 'change process', cooperate in the phases of inception, mobilisation, and goal orientation, the programme will gain momentum within the community. This could be achieved by virtue of the values of the resource group. Creating chances for constant interaction is the most effective means to generate cooperation, and to form viable groups to ensure community participation. Community participation is at the core of any outreach.

Innovativeness: The mind set of the members of a community to create new ideas and the willingness to accept new ideas is an essential value for successful outreach. Those who are not appreciative of change, may refrain from the cause of change. Such a group can never show any favourable attitude towards new ideas and their implementation. So, at least a portion of the group should be inclined towards innovations, if a change is to be introduced. Andrew. J. Sofranko, lists some of the values of the rural people in developing countries as familism, fatalism, low empathy, aversion to risk taking, traditionalism, immediate gratification and submission to nature, etc. He thinks some of these values that need change, could be changed by inducing change incentives such as desire for economic improvement, availability of modern technology, improved extension services, desire for social improvement and expanded opportunities.

Capacity for learning & evaluation: Adoption of updated technologies and latest farm practices are part of any agricultural system. This requires the ability to learn and practice simultaneously. So, the success of outreach depends on i)the capacity of the community for learning and the ability to adopt and ii) the prevalence of the practice of evaluation as an activisor to continue the process. Participatory approach, methods and tools could effectively enhance this capacity, through a 'learning and doing' process.

In a nutshell, well planned mission, organisational efficiency and programmes oriented towards the need of the community, and outreach methods ensuring persistent interactions between the extension personnel and the community of a progressive group of farmers, have culminated in the development of rubber sector. The Outreach of Rubber Board is a model for any development agency.

References

1. Burton, E.Swanson & J.B. Clear, (1984). **Agricultural Extension - A Reference Manual,** Oxford & IBH Publishing Co. New Delhi.
2. Krishna Kumar.A.K. (2002). **A Review of Extension and Development Strategies in Rubber-Rubber Planters' Conference,** India, RRII Publication Kottayam.
3. Krishna Kumar. A.K. (2003). **"India needs advance planning to match growing NR offtake,"** Rubber Asia, 7(2)pp.57-61.
4. Mukundan Menon. P., (2002). **"Natural Rubber in India-Past, Present and Future,"** Rubber Planters' Conference, India, pp17-32
5. A.J. Sofranko (1984).
6. Petty and Cacioppo (1980).

Chapter 19

A Low Cost/No Cost Outreach Model for Rural Development

P.S. Sreekantan Thampi

Extension is a field of professional practice and outreach is a task oriented exercise. Both are powerful and valuable concepts. The challenge of extension is to provide conceptual and leadership base to demonstrate local implications and potential consequences of an interdependent world. Extension now operates in a global village and that our future will be determined in part by the role we choose to play in this larger community.

When the world around us started initiating development processes from the felt needs of society, we a group of like-minded people in a village in Alleppey district of Kerala felt the need to form an organisation with specific tasks to address some of the issues which were given a go by, by the development managers in the region.

The Organisation christened as Jana Jagratha Samithi is registered under charitable societies act and has its declared policies to make outreach in the society without any basic financial resources. To this organisation, the biggest issue that required to be addressed was the need to extend the type of information and technology to the masses it required to reach. As regards finances, the requirement was not felt in the initial phases. Besides, interventions were really possible even without funds. For, resources were available in the form of volunteering and there was the immense possibility of using the local resources without any additional costs.

The agenda before the Jana Jagritha Samithi was to evolve workable models for emulation by task oriented and interested groups of people. Contrary to what is being done by organisations elsewhere, it is not the priority of this organisation to continuously support or stay in stage to perennially empower groups or individuals. The purpose is giving an opportunity, enthuse, motivate to learn and understand, lead them through the first tasks and then scale them up for a while, through promotion for a while, till such time they can stand on their own. But continuing the support for an individual or a group, who cannot sustain or perform, will be a mere waste of time.

Projects that could generate sustainable life patterns, vocations that could help in mending lives of people with average means, organised and group activities that could tender successful results are not often taking place due to the too many political involvements, non-focused government machineries and the high handedness of generalists at the echelons of power. Programmes get started off with lots of fanfare and every programme started gets replaced half-way through, with other populist programmes. The result is duplicating functions, unnecessary asset creations, and too many hands running behind too few margins. This scenario exists in its true formats not only at the State level but also at all the levels of Panchayath Raj set up-at the district, block and village level.

It is in this backdrop that the *Jana Jagratha Samithi* found its formation. The approaches to be made involved at the first stage, addressing the issue at the village level to like-minded people.

The first concept put up for circulation was to have an opportunity for the village men and women and children to come together, to discuss issues of common interest like designing programmes of interaction without vested interests, away from the discrimination of caste, religion and creed, rich and poor, employed and unemployed, officials and non officials, etc.

The second concept was to work for a societal set up to work against the increasing menace of alcoholism and drug abuse.

The third was to reinstate the faith in primary agriculture to develop at least homestead cultivation including cash crops, flowers and livestock.

The fourth was to engineer production and development projects with rapid speed and to generate results. It embraces the aspects of finding out useful income generating employment opportunities/training for skills/ procurement of contracts and orders and stabilising them.

While the first two concepts form part of the extension agenda of the *Samithi,* the third and the fourth were themes for the outreach. It requires to be said here that for the successful execution of these four agendas, it was the will and the involvement that matter and not the funds. One can very well make out the extent of funds required to be spent for these. Funds actually was not needed to set these themes in motion. But if the funds are a matter of concern, yes, then it could be thought so, and then one needs to wait for that.

The operational part of it

The interaction point is taken care of on a regular basis. Talks and discussions on topics of common concern, interactions with personalities that mattered on issues of the current days, orientations and exposure programmes, tours to places where role models perform all these, took place with the active involvement of the participants. Nothing was offered or obtained free and every one participating contributes his or her might.

Alcoholism and drug abuse... the carcinogenic features in any society especially in Kerala, were addressed not directly but through a different approach. People who wanted to actually get rid of such habits were given a helping hand through services of counsellors and doctors. For the rest of them, indirect approaches through meditations and discourses were resorted. The interfaces with other organisations helped a lot in changing the habits of many. It was a resolution that the advocates of the *Jana Jagritha Samithi* remain sober for ever.

Rapidity in the work of Samithi is seen in the execution of outreach technologies for promoting primary agriculture in homesteads. Series of meetings of groups in different localities brought assemblage of people who were open to the concepts of vermin compositing, vegetable growing, cultivation of flower varieties for marketing, growing of ideal cash crops at least in its nominal form in the homesteads, live stock rearing, etc. To our wonder, the groups of men and women were found sitting in gaze daze while realising the fact that the flowers which they normally found growing wild without any care whatsoever in their gardens would fetch prices in the market. Many of the flowers in the local market there came from distant places like Coimbatore and Thovalai.

The *Samithi's* resource persons (qualified and willing functionaries and experienced farmers) took up the responsibility of giving plant rearing practices and demonstrating them free of cost. Tours were organised to the neighbouring municipalities to interact with men and women growing crops in homestead. These models provoked many a souls to start farming operations. The deals from earth worms (vermin-compost manure Rs. 5 per kg) and (vermin-compost yielding 50 worms paise per worm), the gains in growing marigold (Rs. 25 per kg), jasmine (Rs. 40 per kg.) , "Chicken tail" flowers (English version of the local name *Kozhi poovu*) (Rs. 25 per kg.), and indigenous flowers (Rs. 30 per kg.) were made known to them. The village flower shops started procuring the flowers besides the local temples.

Over 20,000 types of seedlings were made available to interested individuals in different localities. It was not a difficult task in organising seedlings, since these are locally available and it was only a question of sourcing them and managing the nursery scientifically. Approaches to companies dealing in flower extracts has helped in getting better flower seed materials. The world's famous McCormicks has its Indian out fit in Cochin, AVT McComicks provided good quality marigold seeds free of cost for this social cause. Some have reaped the first lot of gains and left it then. There are many who still continue to do it as an income supplementing exercise.

Notable task now being undertaken is the planting of pepper trees. Many of the homesteads have lots of trees which are just grown for shade. The *Samithi* has coined a slogan "One tree, One vine" to promote trailing of pepper in all the trees. The motive is to use the otherwise only shade giving tree usefully and profitably to grow pepper which can yield five kgs of green pepper (three kgs of black pepper) at the third year of planting. With just a meager cost of cultivation, the planter can fetch easily Rs. 65 to Rs. 70 per kg. of black pepper. While some of the pepper cuttings were made available to the farmers for a nominal price of Re. 1 per seedling (farmers paid for it), good number of cuttings are now being developed by the activists of the *Samithi* in their own homesteads. This will ultimately turn out to be an income generating exercise for those who make the cuttings also. Expertise is made available to the growers by experienced farmers and willing agricultural officers.

By working in close association with the milk producers society in the region, programmes to enthuse farmers to resort to livestock is also being promoted. Talks and deliberations are being organised at no cost for the farmers. The ultimate aim is to bring in more people in the fold of cow and other homestead animal rearing activity. Discussions often instill confidence in their minds to start animal rearing proposals. To sustain the momentum, the workers of the *Samithi* make it a point to undertake visits to the houses of the farmers. These visits are often found to be encouraging and liked by the actual farmers and instill in them a feeling of partnership.

The fast phase of the activity of the *Samithi* is more discernible in the visualisation, conceptualisation, implementation and stabilisation of certain projects at no cost so to say using local capabilities and talents (available but not utilised properly) and local resources. Tissues and yarn from the plantain stem, fibre from "Potta grass" (grows wild in the now barren paddy fields) are an excellent natural fibres. These are available in large quantities. In order to harness the local resources and the idling housewives and other women population (who remain idle after their daily house chores) were chosen after ascertaining their willingness.

Experts were brought from fibre training centres for training for which actual tuition fees and cost of the material for training were met by the trainees. A batch of 150 women got trained in the making of lot of handicrafts items like table, door and wall mats, tea cup coasters, shopping and fancy bags, caps, other decorative pieces including water paper bins and after the completion of the programme, an order from a Bangalore based exporter was executed with a great success. The women who were involved in the execution of the work were paid for their work from the entire lot of the sales proceeds.

However, the *Samithi* could show that a project of this sort could work well successfully without any outside sourcing. The *Samithi* is now engaged in promoting individuals to take on this for future too. The *Samithi* has no plans to continue this work of permanent support, for it is not in our mandate to shell out charity.

A new project to turn out banana yarns is in the pipline. The *Samithi* has fabricated a tool for the extraction of the yarn. A working woman can make a kg of banana yarn or from any other plantain variety, one kg each a day which can fetch a revenue of Rs. 80 per kg. The upstream Coir and coir exporting companies require huge quantities of this yarn and those who work can surely be confirmed of a revenue. The *Samithi* will soon initiate a first lot exercise of providing a quantity of this fibre to an exporter to prove the workability and viability of this project.

To make use of the kitchen waste and other biological wastes originating from the kitchen, the Samithi decided to advocate setting up of biogas plants. A team of seven volunteers were sent for training in Cochin in the facility of Biotech, an organisation under the Union Ministry of Non Conventional Energy. Of the trained, two women turned active and installed four plants in the neighbourhood. More orders are in the offing since the installed plants are found to be viable and useful in generating the gas for cooking when the LPG cylinder prices are scaling up.

A prestigious outreach achievement is in the crusade against plastics. The *Samithi* leaders had lot of interactions with experts in the line of production and a suitable work kit was developed in house. Training free of cost was imparted to interested women and on completion, two fairly good orders were obtained for supply of paper bags made of out craft paper for a saree fair in a boutique shop in Kottayam and for a Singapore based textile firm. A new order for smaller sample bags have also come in from Sydney, Australia. Half a dozen women work in this segment and they earn a fairly good return from the bag making. Yes, this too is viable in Kerala where many things have turned out to be success at the opening day and winds it way off in due course.

The networking and interlinking with Social work institutes like the Rajagiri College of Social Sciences, Kalamassery, Cochin, Viswagaji Mutt of Muhamma,

Alleppey, Women Initiative Network (WIN Centre) Centre, Eramalloor in Alleppey district, Energy Conservation Society Kerala, AVT MCcormicks, Cochin, Spices Board, Farm Information Bureau, Aswas, an organisation of single women in Cochin, Television Channels especially the Jeevan Television network, newspapers etc have contributed a lot for the success of the Outreach of the *Jana Jagritha Samithi.*

The outreach of this Samithi could work well due to the following:

1. Flexibility in operation
2. Zero investment
3. No financial bondages/tags
4. Beneficiaries made partners in the process through their financial involvement like meeting costs of training and inputs.
5. Best tapping of *Samithi* functionaries' contacts
6. Interlinking and networking with other NGOs.
7. Less dependence on Governmental agencies.
8. Purpose driven activities
9. Result oriented.
10. Less of philosophy and more of actions.

Chapter 20

A Micro Soft Approach to Rural Development

M.P. Boraian

Community Outreach

Colleges and Universities across the countries have 'Community outreach' as a critical component of their off campus activities. *Shramdan*, blood donation, population education, planting of seedlings, literacy, group formation, surveys, supplementary education, *yoga*, cultural programmes, leadership building, resource mobilisation, awareness generation, motivation and counselling are source among the galaxies of programmes undertaken by the teachers and students during their camp in villages and slums.

Most of these programmes turn out to be a one shot affair with a 'hit_and go' approach by the student campers. Programmes with long term vision and lasting benefits to the community and an in-built component of sustainability are very few and far between. In order to break this stereotype rural experience programme of millions of educational institutions across the globe, a new outreach methodology is suggested.

Strategy

Survey: Initially, a wholistic survey of a backward community where the students wish to initiate their outreach programmes during a semester can be undertaken by the entire class or department. The survey can focus upon the existing socio-cultural milieu and the problems confronting the community. For each problem identified by the community, a small group of about two or three persons from the local community, who are knowledgeable about the problem identified, can be requested to be the members of a Task Force constituted by the larger community. Students of a department from a college or a University can be grouped into a small team of two or three, based on the size of the community and magnitude of the problem identified by them for their outreach programme.

The Problem: Similarly, a problem identified should be such that concerted efforts by a small a team of people and students would help find solution in a short duration of about a few weeks or one or two months. Such problems could be either development/welfare oriented or social issue based, which affect the larger interests of the community. These problems should be such that they can be solved by giving representation, visiting government departments/institutions, meeting officials/experts and mobilising local and external resources.

Task Force: Students who are either knowledgeable about or interested in tackling a particular problem can be made members of such committees. With an informed group of local community members and interested group of students, comprising about half a dozen from both the sides, can be entrusted with the task of solving the problems facing the community. Task forces should be formed for attacking common problems or those which affect a group or cluster of the community. Individual problems which are of humane concern could also be taken up for redressal.

Involvement of CBOs: Constitution of various task force committees for solving a set of different problems should have the sanction of local panchayat, self help groups or a youth club, so that it will derive greater strength and stability in its pursuits: Soon after the formation of such committees, a teacher or a faculty member with experience or expertise or interest in the intervention of a select problem may be made an advisor of such committees.

Guidance and Monitoring: Once this tripartite team is built up, the respective committees can meet on a particular day within the community. Teachers who can contribute their mite to more than one committee may do so at this meeting. The President or a Ward member or a Councillor, the head of the college/university or its department and wherever possible, the head of an NGO which has been operating in the local community may form the Guidance and Monitoring Team for all the Task Force Committees in a particular hamlet or village or a cluster. This team will guide, liaise and lead all the committees till they succeed in their mission.

Action Plan: On the day of meeting by all the committees in the community, every committee may come up with an Action Plan of how to go about the entire process of tackling the problem identified. All the committees should provide answer to a common set of questions: what to do, where to do, when to do, how to do, for how long, who will do what, where to go, whom to meet, when to meet and the expenses required in executing the action plan. Whenever the team goes to meet officials, it is necessary that the students team takes the village representatives without fail. The question of cost sharing on such visits should have to be finalised on the day of formulating their action plan.

Cost Sharing: Financial burden of all the Committees will have to be borne locally. Wherever the college or university can take care of the entire or part of the expenses, they can do so. The NGO operating in such communities should be willing to contribute from its funds generously.

The experience of Gandhigram University

Extension Education Department of the Gandhigram Rural University constituted about half a dozen such committees for making sincere efforts towards solving six select problems identified by the local community in its rural neighbourhood. Veterinary care for milch animals, energisation of pump-set for the community overhead tank, transportation to the nearby town, feasibility of starting a dairy cooperative for the self help groups, motivation of the women to use the local community toilet and deepening of a local tank were the issues identified.

These tasks identified by the department in one of the service villages, were entrusted to specific Task Force committees constituted in the above manner. These tasks could be classified into three patterns. Tasks on feasibility study could be done by students and teachers themselves, including the local villagers. Motivation of women for using the community toilet could be done by the students and the local leaders within the community. Veterinary care, energisation of pumpsets, transportation, starting a dairy cooperative had to be done by visiting the respective government departments such as Veterinary Department, Electricity Board, Transport Corporation, Cooperative Milk Union, and Agriculture Engineering Department. While some problems could be solved within a few weeks, others took months, the problem of transportation defied any solution even after three months.

Normally, the students team was able to sort out the solutions to various problems they had identified initially. Experience of Gandhigram University shows that the various student teams achieved their mission by the end of a semester. Wherever it protracted, the same team continued its task in the next semester or handed over to their juniors if they were in their terminal year. Switching over from one village to the other by the end of a semester or a year is left to the college/university, depending upon how far they succeeded and how many problems await solution in the first village.

Assessment: Selection of villages and identification of problems depend on the type of courses pursued by the students. The interest of agriculture, veterinary, engineering, polytechnic, science or social science students will be bound to vary. Students involvement in the community outreach activities could be scheduled in week ends (if necessary including Fridays in a fortnight or a month) so as to enable the teams to visit government departments for taking up the issue.

Teacher advisors in the respective teams should train the students to document their work and allot credits for their labour, regardless of whether they solved the problem or failed due to impediments from officials. The yardstick in judging the work of the student team should not be by its success but by the struggle they had put up in solving the problem.

Review and Documentation: There should be an opportunity to review the work of all the teams in the middle of their mission and towards the end. Periodic sharing and proper documentation of their efforts will pay rich dividends to the students and teachers both academically and in their actual life.

Relating the field experience of various teams in their reviews, with the teaching of theories in classroom by the teachers would make their education more lively and interesting. Such an experiment by all the colleges/ universities will make education socially relevant and academically rewarding. Since the whole exercise is aimed at solution oriented field training at the micro level, it could be called as a micro soft approach (micro level, solution oriented field training).

Conclusion

Academic institutions, village panchayats, NGOs, donor agencies, and the government may encourage this micro soft approach in such a way that it forms an essential component of every one of these institutions. University Grants Commission may strengthen the third dimension of extension, by encouraging all the colleges/universities to follow the micro soft approach in their neighbourhood communities.

Chapter 21

A Community – based Diabetes Education and Nutrition Programme

Padmini Balagopal, N. Kamalamma and Ranjita Misra

Introduction

Diabetes Mellitus will have to be given top billing in the list of today's threats to health. What was once a wealthy man's affliction has now spread to all levels of society. The bad news is that it is increasing, but the good news is that it can be prevented or at worst, delayed even with simple, easy and effective steps like lifestyle modifications.

But in health education issues, one of the most difficult and challenging of issues is to motivate people to change their behaviour even if the message is to optimise health status and benefit from it. It is even more difficult for this changed behaviour to be maintained on a long-term basis. The individual must believe in the Health Belief Model – that he/she believes in health; that he/she is vulnerable to health problems; that such a problem could be serious, and finally, that a health education programme can indeed benefit him/her. When all these beliefs are met, only then will that individual finally take the steps that could optimise health.

In turn, any health education programme, to be effective, must pay attention to the individuality, receptivity, readiness and capability of the target group so that they can be factored into educational sessions. Once the target population is convinced about the inherent benefits from a change of behaviour, successful implementation, adoption and longitudinal maintenance become easier. The health education programme can use the various stages of the Transtheoretical stages of Changes Model as a template to plan and deliver appropriate messages to the target group.

Such a programme was initiated in Gandhigram Rural University under the aegis of the Diabetes Prevention Research Study in the Department of Home Science. This programme was designed to deliver important lifestyle modification changes on Diabetes Prevention to Alamarathupatti village in Dindigul District, Tamil Nadu, India. The rapport that is developed between different members of a homogeneous group was tapped by selecting locally elected Self-Help Group Leaders to deliver health and nutrition messages.

Background

Type 2 Diabetes Mellitus disproportionately affects Indians and is a major public health problem. The prevalence of diabetes has doubled in both rural and urban areas of India during the last two decades. Population growth, genetic predisposition, high illiteracy rate, poverty, and sociological changes that impact lifestyle behaviours have been implication in the etiology and increase of this disease in India. According to the World Health Organisation (WHO) projections, the greatest increase (195 per cent) in the number of type 2 diabetics between 1995 and 2025 is expected to occur in India. At the rate of the present growth by the year 2025, India is projected to have the highest number of type 2 diabetics (57 million), followed by China (38 million) and the U.S.A. (22 million). Health education is one of the most effective public health strategies to prevent the early onset of diseases, and hence is the main thrust of this study is primary prevention. Clinical and biochemical markers specific to an Indian diabetic patient prototype include:

a. a high proportion of central obesity
b. accompanying hyperinsulinemia and insulin resistance
c. presence of dyslipemia and
d. hyperglycemia. The pre-diabetes stage of Impaired Glucose Tolerance (IGT) is also high in India.

A specific and culturally appropriate prevention and self-management strategy for Indians does not exist. Westernisation plays a role in bringing out underlying susceptibility of diabetes (Fujimoto *et al.* 2000)

Purpose of the Study

The primary purpose of this pilot project was to determine if a concentrated diabetes education intervention programme can prevent/delay the early onset of diabetes in an at-risk rural population in India. The secondary objective was to get baseline information on the prevalence rate of diabetes, obesity, and nutritional status among Indian males and females.

Study Site

The village of Aalamarathupatti, part of the extension programmes infrastructure of Gandhigram Rural university, Tamil Nadu was selected as the site for this study. Graduate students were trained to conduct face-to-face interviews prior to the intervention programme. The vital force of Self-Help Group Leaders was also tapped and they were trained and empowered with Diabetes Awareness information. All the members were trained in effective teaching strategies. Pre- and post-data collection were completed so that appropriate parameters could be studied.

Intervention

Intensive diabetes and nutrition education programme was provided tor 7 months. The intervention comprised of a multi-pronged education of the villagers and their families at various level e.g., empowerment techniques (e.g. Self-Help Groups) and education programmes (as part of the graduate student's internship and coursework in the department of Nutrition & Dietetics through the University), to provide a continuity of the thrust on an ongoing basis. Nutrition education sessions included a focus on the use pf high fibre foods, improving a refined cereal diet with the inclusion of food items like sprouted legumes and/or vegetables and the inclusion of an active exercise routine along with stress relaxation techniques. These topics were addressed with the help of teaching aids that included cooking demonstrations, recipe contests, public meetings, folk competitions, model meals and one-one culturally-relevant interviews by trained personnel.

Data collection

Information was collected via face-to-face interviews. Trained interviewers (graduate students and field workers from the University) interviewed those who agreed to participate and signed the informed consent form. Fourteen graduate students in the Department of Home Science were trained for this study. Consent for participation was obtained prior to the interview (the only exclusion criterion was respondent's age <10 years). The sample comprised of the population of an entire village (Aalamarathupatti) above 10 years of age. Sample included adults, pre-menopausal women of child bearing age, and children over 10 years of age. Of the 1100 villagers, 703 respondents (>10 years) were included in this study.

Parameters studied

Height, Weight, Waist-Hip ratio, Body Mass Index (BMI), fasting and post-prandial blood glucose, and blood pressure readings were taken prior to education sessions and they were re-tested at the end of the intervention. Pre- and post-test measurements of dietary intake (calories, protein, dietary fiber, dietary fat) and exercise/physical activity level was measured. Demographic characteristics included age, gender, marital status, education and income level.

Demographic Characteristics

Respondents had a mean age of 36 years (SD=17). Mean educational level was 8th grade. Average family income level was Rs. 838.00 per month (SD=1, 448) (comparable to $18.62). The majority of the respondents were females (58 per cent) and married (95 per cent). Mean Body Mass Index (BMI) of the respondents were in the normal levels (20.3) but 10 per cent were obese/overweight, based on the WHO criteria for Asians (BMI ³ 23.0). Abdominal obesity was prevalent at a much higher degree with 14 per cent of respondents falling in the abnormal range. 27.8 per cent of adults had hyper tension with 4.7 per cent having low blood pressure.

Prevalence Rate

Prevalence rate of diabetes prior to the intervention was 4.7 per cent with Impaired Fasting Glucose (IFG) at 3.2. per cent. Chi-square test showed a positive association between age and blood glucose levels (x^2=73.5, p<0.001). Fasting blood sugar level was significantly (and positively) correlated with respondent's age, blood pressure, and BMI but not their waist-hip-ratio.

Impact of Nutritional Intervention

Intensive diabetes and nutrition education had positive effects in improving the respondent's nutritional intake. Difference I pre- and post-test scores indicated that intake of protein increased (t=2.11, p=0.035), fat / saturated fat decreased (t=10.19, p<.001), and dietary fiber increased (t=10.32, p<0.001) significantly. Reliability of improved nutritional intake, i.e. increased protein & fiber intake, and reduced fat intake was also assessed from the post education responses and unannounced observations at mealtimes.

Blood Glucose Level

The intervention was particularly successful in reducing serum blood glucose levels, both fasting (t=2.87, p=0.006) and postprandial (t=1.99, p=0.049) in the diabetic and IFG groups. There was also improvement in their dietary intake of fiber and protein while lowering the intake of fat/ saturated fat and calories ($p<0.05$). Intervention also had positive effects in reducing respondent's BMI (t=3.21, p=0.001).

Conclusion

Type 2 Diabetes Mellitus is becoming one of the most widespread and deadly diseases in today's world. It is also one of the most preventable of the Diabetes Mellitus diseases. However, it has complex spread to alarming proportions in a development country like India, where health costs are often beyond the reach of the common man. Every effort must be made to stem the onslaught of this debilitating chronic disease both in urban and rural India. A multi-pronged educational approach will help not only in kindling an awareness but also in empowering a population to help prevent high risk populations from developing this disease. The Self-Help Group Leaders of every village should be harnessed as spokes people and empowered messengers to impart education and bring about behaviour and lifestyle modifications.

This study has shown that a focused, intensive and culturally relevant education programme was effective not only in significantly reducing blood glucose levels (among the people with diabetes and IFG group) but also in improving the nutritional intake.

As more than 70 per cent of India is still rural, community SHG Leaders in rural areas are fast becoming the latest battalion to fight and win this growing epidemic.

Chapter 22

Outreach through Training of SHG Women

K. Manikandan and A. Easwaran

Introduction

The recent attempt of Gandhigram Rural University (GRU) in organising three months training on SHG management for rural youth was different from the traditional approaches and methods. It centered around participatory approaches and methods with semi-structured training design. It aims to present and analyse the entire process, management and outcome of the training programme and to draw lessons for similar endeavours.

This work is divided into four major sections. The background of the training programme is given in section one. In section two, the entire training process is presented. Section three presents the outcome of the training. Section four brings out the lessons from the training and wraps up with a conclusion.

Background

Objectives of Training

Based on felt needs, five general objectives were formulated as follows.

1. to organise SHGs in the villages
2. to train the SHG members in managing the activities efficiently
3. to know the ways and means of starting micro-enterprises
4. to initiate efforts to sustain the activities of the SHGs; and

5. to strengthen the socio-psychological and human relation aspects of the group.

The main focus was to bring about positive changes in the knowledge, attitude and skills of the trainees.

Venue of Training: The venue located in a central place, at Gandhigram, in a pleasant atmosphere surrounded by trees and with sufficient space for group exercises ensured a conducive training environment.

Training Design: By and large, it was a semi-structured training design with sufficient flexibility for accommodating trainees' interest. The training contents were arranged in a logical sequence, so as to enable the trainees to get inputs systematically. The subject matter was sufficiently reinforced with theoretical exposure and practical experiences.

Profile of Trainees: The 25 trainees selected were from 12 villages located within 15 km. radius from the training centre of GRU. Among them, a majority were Hindus (88 per cent); more than half of them belonged to Scheduled Caste (52 per cent); and the remaining belonged to Backward Community (36 per cent); and others (12 per cent).

The majority of trainees were females (80 per cent); married (76 per cent); and had two to four members in their family. Sixty per cent were members of SHGs, and the remaining (40 per cent) were not SHG members but had inclination to organise/promote SHGs. All the trainees were literate and among them, those who studied upto 8th standard and above were predominant.

More than half of the trainees depended on petty trade/ business (52 per cent) for their livelihood and the rest were agricultural labourers (44 per cent) and farmers. All the trainees were in the productive age group of 40 years and below. The annual income of the trainees ranged between Rs. 6000 and Rs. 18,000.

The Organisers and Trainers

On the whole, 46 resource persons handled various sessions of the training. They were mostly drawn from the teaching faculties of GRI. Representatives of Gandhigram Trust and other NGOs, banks, panchayt union, cooperative societies, sub-registrar's office, District Rural Development Agencies (DRDA) Tamil Nadu Corporation for Development of Women (TNCDW), District Industries Centre (DIC), Khadhi and Village Industries Commission (KVIC), and Employment exchange also handled sessions.

Financial Profile

A sum of Rs. 2,32,659 was spent for the training programme. The contribution of National Council of Rural Institutes (NCRI) was Rs. 72,451 (31.1per cent) and the rest came from GRU in the form of organisers' salary and provision of infrastructure facilities.

Nearly fifty per cent of the training fund was utilised for paying honorarium of the trainees, and salary and allowances to the organisers of the training. Another 31.2 per cent of the fund was spent for the trainees' stipend, refreshments and vehicle charges for field trips and reading materials. The remaining fund was used for the rent of the training hall and miscellaneous expenditures. The ratio of fund utilised between the trainers, trainees and miscellaneous items worked out to be around 5:3:2. The average training cost of a trainee per day was Rs.124 of which Rs. 30 went to them as stipend.

The Process of Training

In this section, the entire process of training is presented under three heads *viz.*, pre training, training and post training phases.

1. Pre-training Phase

Selection of Trainees

After discussion the training team came out with a set of criteria to select suitable participants for the training. One month before the training, applications were invited from interested participants.

Finally, 25 candidates out of 67 who were really interested were selected.

Training Needs Assessment

Two days before the commencement of the training programme, a pre-training meeting of the trainees and organisers was convened. At this meeting, the issues related to the training programme were analysed in detail and the training needs were assessed. The trainees were sentisitised to function in accordance with the training plan. The expectations of majority of the trainees were: improving the capacity in SHG management and getting training in micro enterprises.

Content of Training

The seven training modules prepared were the subject content of the training programme. Based on the pre-training expectations of trainees, some more topics were included in the training. They covered the training needs of both individual and group, focussed on enhancing capacity and achieving the objectives of training programme.

2. Training Phase

Training Methods

The methods employed in the training were predominantly participatory and trainee dominated. Starting from short lectures and extension talks upto conducting model training in the villages by trainees, many methods were used. Some of the important methods used in the training programme are presented in Box 1.

Training methods adopted

• short lectures • extension talk • method demonstrations • story telling • question answer method • group discussion • group games	• buzz sessions • guided self study • quiz sessions • sharing experience • field visits • case study • group assignments	• laboratory exercise • micro teaching • conducting model training • debate • home work and assignments • learning by doing • back home application

The training methods were planned and combined in such a way that in the early days of training, trainer dominated methods were used. Later, the trainers' role was minimised to the level of catalyst and helper and finally, it was switched over to trainee dominated methods.

On the whole, the emphasis was largely on participatory methods to maximize the involvement of trainees. Certain subjects were repeated using multi-methods to enhance the learning process.

Practical and Field Activities

The trainees were given ample opportunities to learn and acquire skills in data gathering and analysis through Participatory Rural Appraisal (PRA), reporting, convening meetings, enacting dramas, formulating micro-projects, and production and marketing strategies..

As a laboratory exercise, two pilot SHGs were formed among the trainees during training. The trainees operated them for two a months period. This helped them to learn practically the whole process of SHG from its inception to normalisation phase.

Monitoring and Evaluation Mechanism

The training programme was closely monitored and periodically evaluated. The monitoring and evaluation were both internal and external and mostly participatory in nature. The performance of trainees was assessed periodically through written and practical tests and the progress was announced to them immediately.

The performance of trainees in areas like behavioural and attitudinal changes were evaluated at periodic intervals using a variety of tools like quiz, group reporting, assignment, home work, self assessment, ranking by themselves and by co-trainees, trainers' opinion, review of back home application, etc.

The monitoring and evaluation system was kept transparent as it was participatory in nature. It helped in improving the quality of training programme to a great extent.

3. Post-Training Phase

After training, on the last Saturday of every month (over a period of six months) the trainees and organisers assembled for review meeting. In the review meetings, field experiences and practical difficulties of the trainees were discussed and they were re-energised and guided to pursue their work. After one year, the course coordinator met the trainees at their doorsteps and collected information on their back home applications and other impact of the training.

The Outcome of Training

This section concentrates on the assessment of the trainees' state of knowledge, attitude, behaviour and skill in the beginning, at the end and also the status one year after the completion of training.

State of mind of trainees on the first and last day

Table 2 presents the trainees' opinion about their state of mind on the first and last day of the training programme.

On the first day of the training, all the trainees were pre-occupied with a variety of thoughts and all of them were under the impression that they were going to be treated like school students in the training. Some of them felt happy for getting selected for the training. For some trainees, it reminded them of their school days, and some had the feeling of attending college. A section of them had fear, hesitation, and inferiority complex in their mind.

Table 2

State of Mind of the Trainees

On the first day	On the last day
Fear of receiving treatment like school students	Initial fear vanished
Had shivering and hesitation	Unable to digest departing Co-trainees
Felt lucky for getting selection	Became sociable
Reminded of school days	Became self confident
Had inferiority complex and fear	The dream starting a self-employment got strengthened
Silent observation	Felt lucky for getting training
Curious to know about training and felt happy like attending a college	Job seeking desire got intensified
Back home thoughts predominated	Became knowledgeable on SHG and life

It is also clear from the table that on the last day of training, some of their initial fear and prejudices over the training programme had vanished. Most of them became sociable, self-confident and knowledgeable on SHG and had learnt many useful things about life. Their urge for employment and starting self employment got intensified; and most of them were unable to bear their departure from Gandhigram.

Attitude and behaviour changes and skills acquired

The training had resulted in many positive attitudinal changes among the trainees as can be seen in Table 3. The box also lists the skills acquired by trainees including forming and operating SHGs. On the whole, the three months training programme had changed their attitude and behaviour and equipped them with many skills for their personal, family and SHG development.

Table 3

Attitude and Behaviour Change and Skills acquired by the Trainees

Attitudes and Behaviour	Skills
Saving habit	Forming and running SHGs
Reading, writing habits	Organizing meetings, coordinating group activities, motivating SHG members
Habit of pre-planning	Book-keeping and accounting, documentation and report writing documenting minutes
Transparency and frankness	Conducting training
Boldness	Conducting survey, PRA exercise,
Service mindedness,	Communication skills
Emotional control	Making candles, toys, production of washing and cleaning powder
Positive thinking	Rapport building and mobilizing people
Leadership qualities	Preparing project proposals, and marketing skills
Accommodating other interests and patience	Conflict resolution
Adjusting to the environment,	Social work
Self awareness and alertness	Family management
Matured talk and behaviour	
Tolerance	
Freed from prejudice against male	
Cooperative thinking, collective action	
Self confidence	

Feedback from others

The trainees received positive feedback from their parents/ husbands and fellow villagers on their performance. The parents/ husbands of trainees felt happy about their wards after noticing improvement in them. The friends of most trainees appreciated them on seeing improvements. The villagers who observed the training appreciated the performance of trainees.

The feedback from many quarters shows that the three months training was effective and useful to them. The training was successful in fulfilling training needs and expectations.

Status of Trainees after one year

Table 4 gives the status of trainees as a result of the training. All the trainees reported that they were sustaining the positive attitude and behaviour changes acquired from the training.

On the whole, it may be stated that almost all the trainees were utilising the training input for their betterment in different ways. It could also be stated that the three months training on management of SHGs offered by GRU for the 25 village youths was effective.

Conclusion

It may be concluded that the three months training on SHG management tried to shift the emphasis from authoritarian to democratic approaches, centralisation to decentralised management, and from imparting mere theoretical knowledge to practical application of the learning in the field. Today, SHGs are growing rapidly and enormous government funds and other resources are flowing into them. It is the most appropriate time to equip the SHG functionaries to make use of the resources efficiently. In this context, apart from Government, the higher educational institutions, research and training institutions and NGOs have a key role to play.

Table 4

Status of the trainees one year after the training

Sl. No	Status after one year	No. of Responses	%
1.	Sustaining the attitude and behaviour changes acquired From the training	25	100
2.	Improved social status	19	76
3.	Maintaining close contact with co-trainees	14	56
4.	Started to lead a planned life	13	52
5.	Became in-charge for maintaining SHG accounts, Improved the SHG, got revolving fund, involved in some social service, increased family income	13	52
6.	Became SHG president	11	44
7.	Secured employment (NGO & private)	10	40
8.	Started self employment	9	36
9.	Trained SHG members	6	24
10.	Started SHGs	3	12
11.	Selected as ward member in village panchayat	3	12
12.	Became SHG federation president	2	8
13.	Became executive member in an NGO	1	4

Notes

1. Chowdhry, P.D., (1986). **Training Methodology and Management,** New Delhi: Sterling Publishers.
2. Singh, R.P., (2000). **Management of Training Programmes,** New Delhi: Anmol Publications Pvt. Ltd.
3. Narayanasamy, N., *et al.* (2001). **Management of Self Help Groups: A Handbook for the Trainers,** GRU, Gandhigram.
4. *Ibid.,* p.12
5. Lynton, R.P., and Pareek, U., (2003). **Training for Development,** New Delhi: Vistaar Publications.

Chapter 23

Outreach by SHG Women through Rural Marketing

C. Krishnasamy

Gandhigram has been involved in various aspects of rural development for the past 58 years. The activities covered are as follows:

- Social welfare
- Health
- Education
- Employment generation
- Extension activities
- Research and development in appropriate technologies

Objectives

- Rural employment
- Rural industrialisation
- Productive usages of finance, credit and local savings
- Encouraging local level sustainable entrepreneurship
- Designing and implementing the substantial and constructive role for women SHGs

The current development strategy

Over the years, there has been a shift in our involvement practices. We began with going to the village and reaching out to the villager as individuals. Soon we recognised and accepted the limitation of this strategy. We felt we needed to design systematic intervention strategies via Khadi, Education, and Health, etc. to deliver the developmental benefits. Today, we seem to have a full circle *albeit* with a qualitative difference. In the villages, we have like minded SHGs which can be the vehicles to deliver development benefits. Of course, they will partake of the same too. And on our part, we need to redefine our facilitator's role.

SHGs at Gandhigram

Gandhigram Trust has promoted 150 SHGs in Dindigul, Theni and Tirunelveli District. These SHGs are helped by DRDA, Tamil Nadu Women Development Corporation and local financial institutions. These SHGs are involved in savings and credit for more than seven years. Having gained the financial, administrative experience, they are relieved from the clutches of money lenders. These women have been empowered through various motivations. They have made useful contribution in the *Grama sabhas*, SHG activities, micro enterprises activities and individual entrepreneurship. At present, these SHGs at panchayat level have formed a federation and registered under the Trust Act. The number of SHGs in a federation varies from 10 to 24. One representative from Gandhigram Trust acts as a facilitator.

All the SHGs are linked with local banks. They have created credibility with banks. Bankers have come forward to finance the SHGs from Rs. 25,000 to Rs. 2.5 lakh per group. Through the motivation of EDP training provided by us with the support of DRDA, DIC, THADCO and Tamil Nadu Women Development Corporation, most of the women SHGs are involved in the enterprising activities such as:

- running of canteen
- flour grinding / mini mill / wet grinding, dough for idlly, dosa
- Photo frame work
- Mushroom cultivation
- Petty shops
- production of eatables
- Herbal collection
- Construction work
- Vermin compost and

Micro enterprises

As part of our Anniversary celebrations during the year 2001, we had an SHGs meet. A few SHG leaders spoke about the need for micro enterprises as they were in the position of creating financial resources. They requested to help them – both in production and marketing.

Gandhigram Trust has always involved the people's participation in any developmental programmes at village level. Accordingly, we prepared a plan of action in a participatory manner as the bottom up approach. Subsequently, we called all the SHGs for preparing a plan of action. Totally, 530 members from the SHGs participated and they gave their ideas on what kind of economic activities they can take up, what would they produce and how would they market it. This approach gave us dividends since rural entrepreneurs were involved right from the planning stage.

The process of planning

The SHG members divided themselves into groups and after some more discussion came out with many ideas about activities and the products. On marketing of village industries products, they gave some practical suggestions. In their own words, "our detergent powder is of good quality but it is available only in 1 kg packet costing Rs.20. Our tooth powder is also available only in 100 gram packs, priced at Rs. 20. In villages, most of us are daily wage earners, getting Rs. 20 to Rs. 60 per day. How can we spend Rs. 20 for detergent or Rs. 20 for tooth powder? Please give us 100 gram pocket of detergent and 10 gram pocket of tooth powder. They identified the following trades which they can take up for production and marketing.

- Pappad making
- Agarbathi
- Detergent and scouring powder
- Catering
- Sanitary napkins
- shampoo making
- cultivation of medicinal plants
- Edible / non edible oil extraction
- Vermi compost
- Masala powder
- Acreca nut leaf plates
- Silk cotton extraction & manufacture of mattresses and pillows
- petty shops (to market the SHGs products & village industries)

Based on their suggestion, we motivated the SHGs to take up the production and marketing activities with the financial support for creating infrastructure and working capital. The like-minded SHGs started their production activities. Initially for the first year, we provided support and guidance for getting quality raw materials, book keeping and accounting. Now, the SHGs have been independently managing their units.

Presently, 11 out of 13 units are successfully running at Gandhigram and in the neighbouring villages (except shampoo making & vermi compost). Through the above units, about 32 women are directly getting regular employment opportunity. In addition, indirect employment has also been generated to members of SHGs towards procuring raw materials such as herbs, neem seeds, silk cotton, etc.

New Marketing Strategy

We selected the potential SHG members through our EDP training for sales representatives. The selected members were given a special package of marketing and salesmanship training for one week as residential programme. In this training, we taught them about the various marketing techniques for rural marketing and ethos of Gandhian philosophy and rural products.

Currently, 61 persons are involved in the marketing of SHGs products and village industry products. The monthly sales touches Rs. 2.5 lakh. Each sales representative has selected 6 to 10 villages around his/her residence. The average monthly sales per person varies from Rs. 5,000 to 18,000. Their earning through sales commission is from Rs.1,500 to 3,600. Apart from these sales representatives the SHGs and Gandhigram Khadi Trust have signed a Memorandum of Understanding for mutually helping in supply of products and marketing. Through this practice, we found that the transfer of management of industry from institution to SHGs is possible. This practice can be replicated at any place according to the availability of local resources and can create local employment in rural industries. This is the dream of constructive programme of Mahatma Gandhi, our father of the Nation.

Chapter 24

Cyber Extension for Transfer of Technology

L. Nirmala and V. Sekar

Transfer of Technology

In the present era of communication, we have developed a lot of agencies for the dissemination of information to farmers. Several efforts have been made by the government and private agencies to speed up the process of transfer of technology so as to narrow down the technological and adoption gap. The latest advances in Information Technology (IT), computers, telecommunications and Internet have provided conducive environment for adopting new technologies and making the method of instructions more effective and interactive.

Internet has become an unavoidable necessity for organisations especially those involved in technology transfer. It enhances the efficiency of implementation. It can also act as a powerful medium for the transfer of modern technology to the farmers. Internet and its application are also very useful in agricultural research, education, extension, planning of crop production, forecasting, post-harvest management; marketing disaster management, etc. Such application of internet would ensure a proper growth of the agricultural sector on a sustainable basis.

Besides, farmers can also benefit directly through the utilisation of various web sites that have been launched by the Government. Generally, the collection of information on various aspects of crops in agriculture is done. Internet websites are another tool for the farmer to acquire information and solution.

In the changed environment of today, the internet has to be given due weightage as a very powerful IT tool for technologies down grass root level. For this, every organisation should try to explore the internet resources and achieve internet connectivity and make the people aware of the important resources and services available. India is a vast country and the need of the hour is to extend this facility to the entire nation, even to the remotest of the region and villages, so that everyone has access to this technology. This technology includes not only web servers and browsers, but the Hypertext Markup Languages (HTML), the Universal Resource Locator (URL), Internet search engines, and back-end service applications. Web provides a new means of accessing information on the Internet. Initially, host computers published information via pages written in HTML.

Why Cyber Extension is Needed Now?

To provide need-based information to farmers, timely solutions to farmers' problems, direct opportunity to interact with the scientists and information at the preferred and convenient time of the farmers.

n-logue's Rural Connectivity Model

n-logue links village kiosks over a 20-km diametre region to a central node, using a low-cost wireless infrastructure. Nodes are then linked to the Internet and the phone system. Shared access at the kiosk and shared spectrum at the central node concentrates digital traffic and ensures high levels of usage and low costs. At the same time, the n-logue approach concentrates the buying power of up 50,000 customers per node, generating high cash flow. Both kiosks and nodes are operated as franchisees by local entrepreneurs.

Services from Kiosk

Services

- Communication services
- Agricultural information
- e-governance
- Education
- Entertainment
- Telephone
- Showing the equipments at best price & quality
- Installing the equipments & training on their use
- Train the operators on Internet usage, marketing & agency business
- Providing quality Internet services
- Identify newer usage & services for rural continuously
- Work with government administration for e-governance

The result is phone and internet service at costs Indian villagers can afford and a business model that looks very robust. Because n-logues' model links the informal and formal economy, the company also helps to sell access to its customers by providing a platform for a wide range of services.

Computer revolution is spreading in every arena of human endeavour *viz.*, in banking, airlines, railways and defense but very little has been done in agriculture sector. To sustain self-sufficiency in food, it is essential that the advancement in IT must be extended to farming community. Areas of usage advanced from computing to the existing multitude of uses in agriculture research such as Decision Support Systems (DSS), Expert Systems (ESS), extension services to farmers, farm management, training, etc.,

Information Technology (IT) with its various tools such as Internet, GIS ESs and DSSs can play a vital role in improving the existing status of the farmers. A range of communication technologies have been developed and are being used to meet the demand of rural population of the country. At present, benefits of IT are available to farming community also. Moreover, improved communication and information access is directly related to socio-economic development. This paper tries to explain that the internet is emerging as a tool with potential to contribute to rural development.

Role of Internet in Agricultural & Rural Development

Services that can be Provided Through Internet:

- Technical information
- Market information
- Weather condition
- National level agricultural events
- State & central Government policies & schemes
- Training calendars
- E-mail & Voice mail services
- Video conferencing

Advantages of Internet Services

- On the spot data availability
- Timely information
- Avoid unnecessary movement of farmers from their places to research centre
- Cost of contact per farmer is reduced

The 'Internet' is a network of networks that connects computers all over the world. Computer is a major component of Information Technology (IT), which is helpful in doing routine things faster, more accurately and leaves us to concentrate on the analysis of the information and take proper decisions.

Chapter 25

Outreach through Watershed Approach: Maladies and Remedies

N.D. Mani

Watershed Approach

A watershed basically comprises drainage line and arable and non-arable lands which are required to be developed in an integrated and holistic manner. In order to ensure optimum use of natural resources and sustainable production, the watershed approach lays stress on the adoption of the watershed area as an organic geo–hydrological unit for planning and implementation through the people, their groups and associations. A micro watershed of about 500 ha. is taken and saturated with soil and water conservation works to promote a suitable and sustainable production system in a four year period.

Central and State governments are turning to watershed approach as a means of achieving greater results from their area development programmes because managing area development programmes on a watershed basis makes good sense - environmentally, financially and socially.

One of the salient features of this approach is people's participation. People's participation leads to greater awareness and participation from the watershed community. Once individuals become aware of and interested in their watershed, they often become more involved in decision-making as well as in protection and restoration efforts. Through such involvement, watershed approach builds a sense of belonging, community ownership, helps to reduce conflicts, and increases commitment to the actions necessary to achieve the objectives of the programme. It strengthens team work, which brings private and public partners together. In the process, all natural resources such as land, water, vegetation and livestock and also people within the watershed get developed.

Problems of Watershed Approach

Administration

The tall administrative structure for watershed development with seven levels starting from State level to watershed level reduces the pace of decision making.

Integrated development of watershed is not given importance because more number of non-technical personnel is associated with technical works and the technical personnel have been asked to take up ministerial work. The Government structure is technically sound at the top level but at the lower level the Watershed Development Team (WDT) has a technical team consisting of young people fresh from colleges, most of whom live outside the watershed. The Government utilises the expertise of its officials in the Distict Watershed Development Advisory Committee (DWDAC) and also while organising training programmes, whereas their expertise is not available at the field level to the extent required for effective implementation of the activities.

Further, the limited capacity and exposure of the project staff to watershed concepts is another limitation. As a result, the crucial activity of soil and water conservation remains an activity of experience, which is not conducive to holistic development. Ridge to valley approach has not been followed during implementation because of involvement of non-technical personnel.

One of the important problems has been the unwillingness of the bureaucratic and Panchayat Raj system to give up control over this programme and to accept new partners and new ways of doing things. Frequent transfer of officials in-charge of the programme and resignation of trained members of WDT hampers the activities.

Awareness Creation and Capacity Building

Watershed approach is a people-centered and people driven one; the stakeholders of the watershed community i.e. Users Groups (UGs) and Self Help Groups (SHGs) were not properly motivated to play an active role. Hence, they have not realised the importance and utility of soil and water conservation in the overall development of watershed. The beneficiaries, though they have a fair idea about the problems and the type of treatment, are not fully conversant with the technicalities of different moisture control and water conservation structures. The beneficiaries were also not trained properly on the practices in the post project period.

People's Participation

Officials involved in the implementation of the programme have not been oriented to work with people and hence have not taken much effort to enlist people's participation in the watershed activities. Due to poor participation of people, local and low-cost technologies were not used.

In many cases, involvement of the people in the identification of location for various project activities has been absent. Hence some of the activities of the programme were not appropriate to the location and many a times, their location is wrong or against the wishes of the farmers and users. The beneficiaries are not involved in the monitoring of activities, as they are not trained to undertake such activities. In general, the community is treated as beneficiaries, but not as stake-holders.

Watersheds are wrongly identified because of the urgency on the part of government for submission of proposal and non-availability of data at village level. Pre-funding studies are rarely conducted in government funded watershed projects.

Functioning of UG

The members of various committees/associations/groups are not motivated to attend the meetings regularly. Consequently, they are not sharing the information and ideas, leading to poor acquisition of knowledge and poor participation in the watershed activities. There is lack of cooperation among the members of UG because of the controversial conversation and thinking among the user groups. The UG members maintain assets created in their lands but they fail to maintain the common assets properly.

Functioning of SHG

SHGs are not effective, mainly due to poor patronage from the PIA/WDT as well as poor participation of its members. Though this programme helped farmers, it could not ensure the fullest participation of the landless and the poor people in the watershed.

Functioning of PIA

In majority of the watersheds, Principal Implementing Agency (PIA) has concentrated only on one or two core activities that too in government lands. The PIA is particular about achievement of targets. In some cases, contractors were also engaged to achieve the physical and financial targets in time. This is true when the funds are released by the end of the financial year. This cuts the very roots of beneficiary - driven and community managed participatory process.

Stakeholders could not get the benefits at the right time and some times, the delay was mainly due to the poor coordination and often delay in the release of funds by the government. The PIA is not able to sustain the initial rapport established with the community in the long run or at least till the end of the programme.

Role of NGO

The NGOs involvement is restricted to the organisation of watershed Community into Watershed Association (WA)/Watershed Committee (WC)/UGs and SHGs and to the training of the watershed community. Their experiences in watershed development have not been utilised and they are seldom involved in the execution of project activities.

Remedies for the Obstacles

Administration

Efforts have to be taken to involve experts from line departments, academic institutions, etc. in the selection of activities, location and supervision of implementation of various components. Government has to make available key officials engaged in the programme execution throughout the programme period.

Awareness should be created among the bureaucrats and *panchayat* leaders on the benefits of entrusting the programme implementation to the community. The members of the WDT have to be given field based training and should execute a bond ensuring their availability during the entire period of the programme. They have to stay in the watershed for more fruitful interaction and supervision.

Awareness Creation and Capacity Building

The awareness building may be strengthened by arranging field visits to model watersheds, publication and distribution of non-technical literature to farmers, and through participatory extra-mural activities. The members of the watershed need training in technical content as well as the skills to recognize and improve upon indigenous technical knowledge. They also need to be trained in PRA methods, community organisation, administrative and accounting procedures and the tools and techniques of project management.

Training packages may be evolved for awareness generation and capacity building. They have to be designed based on the requirements of the beneficiaries and members of WDT. Training institutions may also be identified for developing sufficient training infrastructure facilities. The topics of conflict resolution and group dynamics have to be included in the training module of WDT, UGs and SHGs, for smooth functioning of these bodies and to make them more active in the conflict resolution process.

People's Participation

Adequate efforts have to be taken for enlisting participation of the local people including women, youth and village *panchayat* in the preparation of watershed development plan and activities.

User Groups

The members of UG should be oriented towards maintenance of individual as well as common assets of the programme through a workshop, and be motivated to maintain the resources. The importance of attending meetings should be explained to the members for better understanding and participation in the watershed activities.

SHG

Equal attention has to be paid in the sharing of benefits by all the members of the community in the watersheds. For better participation of poor and landless, all of them have to be organised into SHGs. Additional efforts have to be taken by the PIA, WDT and local panchayat for convergence of other relevant rural development programmes implemented by government and also for finding other sources of finance.

PIA

For holistic development, the PIA has to undertake more number of diverse activities from ridge to valley covering both government and private lands.

Watershed development programme is essentially a process-oriented development rather than event dominant activity. The PIA should follow process approach rather than target approach.

NGOs

NGOs fill the gap between government machinery and the community because they normally work with the village community. NGO functionaries live in the watershed and hence they interact more frequently with the stakeholders. This helps them in achieving the end results/ targets successfully.

Conclusion

Area development programme implemented adopting watershed approach is slowly changing the overall environmental situation in watersheds. However, the impact is not on the envisaged lines mainly due to poor technical input, poor participation of the community and the most important factor is failure of rainfall.

Chapter 26

Reaching out to the Rural Disabled: The Role of a Rural Varsity

M.P.Boraian

Social Responsibility

Universities and Colleges have the social responsibility of serving the weak and vulnerable -individuals, groups and communities in the rural environs of their satellite area. The poor people, *adivasis*, *dalits*, disabled, the aged, destitute women and the diseased (with terminal illness) are the most deserving vulnerable categories among the rural population. Government, Non-Government Organisations, corporates and service clubs do not always cater to such downtrodden and distressed groups in full and address their problems comprehensively. Gandhigram Rural University, as part of its outreach mission in the neighbouring rural communities, ventured to take one of these groups *viz.*, the physically and mentally challenged persons for promoting their welfare and protecting their rights.

Department of Extension Education of the Gandhigram Rural University (GRU), as part of its community service oriented regular extension programmes, surveyed the rural environs of Gandhigram in order to identify the differently abled persons. Nearly 200 differently abled persons with diverse forms of disabilities, (orthopaedically challenged, speech and hearing impaired, visually challenged, mentally challenged and the leprosy cured) comprising men and women, boys and girls, youth and the aged, representing a cross-section of religions and communities comprise the target groups. These groups have been subsisting in the service villages of GRU, sprawling over 10 village *panchayats* in Athoor and Dindigul blocks of Dindigul district, Tamil Nadu.

Initially, a base-line survey was undertaken by the Faculty and students at the doorsteps of all those persons with disabilities, in order to understand their family background, history of disability and their desires and ambitions. The survey revealed that the physically and mentally challenged persons were characterised by poverty, illiteracy, lack of skills, problem of mobility and poor resources to fall back upon. They faced neglect and sarcasm from the society, rejection and ridicule by the prospective employers, subservience and servitude to their supporters and felt resigned to their fate.

Meet for Interaction

Among the numerous problems confronting the Persons with Disabilities (PWDs), the desire to move out of their home at least for a day and interact with people outside their home was more appealing. Hence, a day-long get together was organised at Gandhigram with all these PWDs. Besides fulfilling their interactional desire, this meeting helped to design intervention strategies through collective consultations.

In addition to their interactive opportunities, the meet served a more valuable purpose. Persons with minor disabilities who were resigned to their fate previously, felt relieved and recharged when they saw the others with greater difficulties; so were those with major disabilities when they looked at the severely disabled, brought to the venue only with the help of supporters. The severely disabled too heaved a sigh of relief when they were informed that there were a few chronically bedridden persons, unable to be escorted anywhere outside, but lying at their home for years together.

All the severely disabled and the aged care-givers were brought by the university vehicle from their doorsteps in every village and were safely dropped at home. While many managed to come either on their own or on the pillions of their supporters' vehicle, the mentally retarded and severely disabled persons were escorted to the workshop venue, supported by their parents and care givers. The belief that it will be comfortable for the PWDs to arrange a special vehicle to bring them and drop them back was disproved when the local community witnessed the painful scene whereby the severely disabled persons were virtually packed up and dumped into the bus by their parents and supporters with utmost hardships. Since that was the first time they were moving out of their village by a bus or any automobile in their life time, both the severely disabled and their parents realized the intensity of their transportation problem.

Awareness Meet

Upon successful completion of the workshop, all the participants expressed their need for awareness about the various government schemes benefiting the PWDs. Accordingly, another one day awareness workshop was organised at the Gandhigram Rural University campus. The disabled students pursuing their studies at GRU were also invited to attend the workshop, in order to benefit from the information about welfare schemes shared by the government officials (Project Officer, District Rural Development Agency, and Disabled District Rehabilitation Officer, Government of Tamil Nadu). Besides raising people's awareness, this workshop enabled PWDs from the villages and the disabled students to understand each other's problems and coping strategies. The major outcome of this workshop was the motivation given by the students to the drop out youth from villages and the latter's resolve to resume their studies, upon seeing the interest evinced by the students. On their part, the students realised the difficulties of poor persons among the disabled and imagined the sufferings faced by their parents in educating them.

SHGs for the Disabled

Enthused by the officials' encouragement at the Awareness Raising Workshop to start Self Help Groups (SHGs), in order to become eligible for receiving subsidised loans for starting self employment ventures, Department of Extension Education organised 15 self help groups in various villages-11 among the women and four among the men, with a membership of about 100. It was suffice to have about half a dozen members in each group, unlike the 15-20 member requirement for the regular Self Help Groups, for obvious reasons of the availability of only a limited number of the disabled persons in one location. All these 15 SHGs were linked with the nearby nationalised banks and have been paying a subscription of Rs. 50 per month.

District Rural Development Agency (DRDA) deputed an official to examine the functioning of SHGs for distribution of subsidised loans. In order to be eligible for a group to be supported by the DRDA, it should have atleast a sum of Rs. 5,000 as its resource base. Assuming that a six member SHG pays its subscription regularly every month, an SHG will have a saving of Rs. 3,600 per annum. Since most of the SHGs are struggling to pay their subscription regularly, it will take about three years for a group to be eligible for Government assistance. But, by then, most of the groups are likely to lose interest and leave the groups.

All the SHGs have been awaiting government loans anxiously but there has been a delay due to the change of government after the recent elections and subsequent transfer of officials. In order to mitigate the monetary sufferings of members requiring short credits and recycle the members' savings, the SHGs were allowed to draw from their internal savings at 24 per cent interest for embarking upon small economic ventures of their choice, such as goat rearing, sweet candy making, tea shop, etc.

Challenges of SHGs

Functioning of SHGs has been confronting certain unformidable challenges. Payment of regular subscription for the already poverty stricken disabled members is a serious problem. For members who have been fully dependent on their parents or supporters, this is an impossibility. Then, there are some abandoned young girls and boys who eke out their livelihood through errand jobs or work as child labourers. All the three categories of members manage to pay their subscription with utmost hardship.

Some members who took loans from their group's savings happned to meet with exigencies on health grounds; these members neither repaid their loan nor paid their subscription. Worse, some had to be hospitalised in nearby towns and none went to their rescue. A few lost their homes in a wall collapse during heavy rains and they subsisted in the *verandah* of their neighbours. Such persons have therefore been struggling for their most basic needs-food, shelter, drinking water and domestic lighting, not to talk of health, education, skills and mobility support.

Non-Government Organisations (NGOs) with foreign funds, operating in the same communities, pump in more loans, subsidies and concessions to the Self Help Groups formed by them. When the already struggling SHGs for the disabled look at these fortunate SHGs for the healthy persons, they get frustrated and frown upon the organisers/ convenors. As a result, and with no financial support coming forth from the government, some SHGs in the service villages are on the threshold of folding up. Failure of some members in repaying the groups savings, taken as loans, has been sending a wrong signal to the government officials in sanctioning loans. This has already alerted the other groups, from allowing any internal loans. Moreover, when the formation of fresh group is on the anvil in a village, where such a default was witnessed, the members were wary and reluctant to move ahead.

At this critical juncture, National Thermal Power Corporation (NTPC), a Public Sector undertaking by the Government of India had invited proposals for financial support to the SHGs for the disabled. Applications were. submitted by all the SHGs to NTPC through the Gandhigram Rural University, but in vain.

Disability Certification

Department of Extension Education entered in to another longstanding demand of the disabled i.e. National Disability Identity Certificate, a vital document for every disabled to avail the benefits of all government schemes such as free bus pass, train pass, disability pension, loan with subsidy, supportive devices and equipments and admission and appointment in the government system.

All the disabled persons were brought from their homes to the government hospital at the district headquarters (Dindigul, about 20 kms. away) through a specially arranged vehicle to undergo medical examination. An Expert team comprising specialists in each type of disability (*viz.*, Orthopaedist, Ophthalmologist, ENT, and Psychiatrist), diagnosed the type and level of their disability and issued them disability certificate. The severely disabled persons underwent the agony of getting down from the bus and boarding it again, as the doctors were unwilling to walk down a few metres to examine them inside the bus.

Institutional Linkage

GRU associated itself with a funding agency *viz.*, ADD India (Action on Disability and Development) which organised a training programme on 'Community based rehabilitation' and another one on 'Community mental health' sponsored by Basic Needs India. Also, ADD India organised a training programme in association with the Department of Extension Education for its partner NGOs from various parts of Tamil Nadu, with focus on using Participatory Rural Appraisal (PRA) method in analyzing the problems of the disabled in rural communities. ADD India trained a differently abled Master's students in Rural Project Management from Gandhigram, for internship. The Master students also studied the problems of differently abled persons in all the service villages for their dissertation work.

The department has been scouting for support from specialised service institutions in the nearby towns and cities (Madurai) and linking them up with their respective target groups, for facilitating them to avail the institutional services by the disabled poor. For instance, St. Joseph's School for the Blind at Madurai visited the family of two blind children-a girl and boy aged 3 and 4 respectively (the only two kids to their poor parents from a *dalit* community), and promised to enroll them with free education. In an attempt to establish linkage with regional level institutions overseas, GRU has become an Associate member of the Asia Pacific Centre on Disability (APCD), Bangkok, Thailand.

All these activities have been carried among the physically challenged persons without any additional resources from special projects or budget allocations but only with the infrastructural support extended by the university.

Programmes Envisaged

Department of Extension Education has planned to organise a medical check up for the mentally ill persons, from a network of NGOs working among the disabled, bring all the disabled persons under insurance cover, design mobility devices through GRU's innovation centre, take them out on an exposure to disability related institutions in nearby towns and cities, sponsor the youth to vocational training centres for skill training and undertake other related activities for the welfare of the disabled.

Societal Handicaps

- The physically challenged persons with severe disability are constrained in their mobility, resulting in the very low level of employment, leading to extreme poverty and dependence on their already economically weak families. They are largely neglected by institutions and individuals around them.
- The government follows its routine approach of responding to the represented problems of the disabled persons, subject to their eligibility under the various schemes available, by making them run trom pillar to post, treating them like their healthy counterparts. Government schemes benefited largely those with minor disabilities and hence would bother the officials by their frequent visits to the various government offices.
- Persons with severe disabilities and soaked in poverty or penury could seldom tap the doors of the government. Such critical cases remain uncared for long and have a graceful natural death, wherever they are cared by their loving parents. When the parents or the most loved carers are dead and gone, the severely disabled face the risk of forced mercy killing by the second line carers such as the in-laws. The plight of disabled children, abandoned by their parents, in the name of poverty-induced migration for work in neighbouring states is even more precarious, unable neither to have a dignified living nor have a graceful death.
- Banking and financial institutions are wary of loaning the disabled persons either to the individuals or their self help groups, lest they may default.

- Village panchayats avoid them in registering for unskilled employment under the National Rural Employment Guarantee Scheme, since the manual operations are more demanding and their wage is productivity linked.
- NGOs operating in the project area seem to be more project and result oriented, rather than community and service oriented. Hence, they desist from working with the disabled as their target groups. The corporates largely sponsor or support projects which not only benefit the community but primarily serve the corporate interests as well, either overtly or latently. Neither producers nor consumers, the disabled persons do not come under their commercial criteria. Nor their greatest demand for mobility and assistive devices could be afforded by them.

On the whole, disability of persons spirals the viciousness in every aspect of their life and compounds their distress and agony. They continue to wallow in penury, illiteracy, ignorance, and frustration in life on account of their all round neglect.

Suggestions

Based on our experience, certain suggestions are made in the following paragraphs:

- Since all the SHGs comprise largely the poverty stricken members, payment of subscription or repayment of loan becomes doubly difficult, than for the SHGs with healthy members. Therefore, SHG as a strategy for improving the plight of physically challenged persons needs to be reconsidered by the government and other change agents.
- Government (District Disability Rehabilitation Office) needs to be more concerned about and be proactive in supporting and serving the disabled. Unlike other government departments, District Disability

Rehabilitation team may need to visit at least every panchayat headquarter village, if not to the hamlets and their doorsteps. The benefits and concessions extended by various government departments and government undertakings may be channelised through the District Disability Rehabilitation Office. Instead of making the disabled including the severely disabled to limp and crawl to various government offices, the government may funnel down all the benefits at the *panchayat* level.

- NGOs running homes and hospitals avoid taking the severely disabled persons into their fold, or insist upon a supporter to accompany such persons even for institutionalisation on payment. Very severely disabled persons wailing in their huts or farmsteads, facing the wrath of penury and the risk of forced killing, need to be given special attention by NGOs in caring and hospitalising them on humane grounds.
- Sick persons with disability are forced to ignore health care, which compounds and complicates their already fragile system. Separate health care system should be designed by which mobile team of doctors can visit *panchayat* headquarters periodically for caring all the disabled, particularly those who are diseased and very severely disabled.
- Mobility is a critical need of most of the disabled persons, particularly the school/college goers and persons with distant worksites. Supportive devices such as cycles, wheel chairs, tri-wheelers could be provided to all the disabled, according to their disability. Every school or a college should have the required number of two/three wheelers parked at certain common points such as bus stop, hostel, classroom, laboratory, canteens, computer centres so that any disabled person can easily move about from one place to another at ease and leave their

vehicle wherever they depart from. Similarly, a feasible system has to be designed for the rural disabled, so that they are independent and have a dignified living.

- The home-bound, severely disabled and illiterate persons may be provided with literacy skills and enabled to read local newspapers, magazines and development communication materials relevant to their needs and problems. Skill training is another critical input badly needed by persons with potential and interest, but mired in poverty and penury. Government, in partnership with NGOs, may therefore sponsor literacy and skill training programmes together.
- Insurance companies may devise schemes by which they bring all the poor disabled, under free insurance cover or subsidised premium. Disabled persons from better economic condition could also be covered under similar schemes with differential rates of premium. Parents of the very severely disabled and the mentally disordered persons could also be benefited by the insurance companies suitably.

Chapter 27

Outreach by a Veterinary University among the Livestock Farmers

P. Mathialagan and A. Manivannan

Outreach Programmes

Tamil Nadu Veterinary University (TANUVAS) caters to the needs of the farming community by reaching out to them through its constituent extension centres and colleges. A chain of sixteen Veterinary University Training and Research Centres, three Farmers Training Centres, two Krishi Vigyan Kendras and one Agricultural Technology Information Centre are located in various districts of the entire state for creating proper link between the research workers and the end users.

The programmes undertaken by the above centres include training unemployed youths, women, school drop-outs, and practicing farmers towards establishing livestock and fisheries enterprises, providing advisory services, and dissemination of technology through mass media, distance education and demonstrations. Dissemination of technical know-how by way of farm radio schools, TV programmes, press releases, popular bulletins, folders, pamphlets, books, journals and news letters are carried out regularly.

Entrepreneurship Development Cell caters to the need for raising awareness and also imparting skill training for developing entrepreneurs on livestock and fisheries. Courses are conducted at district centres on livestock and fisheries-related product technology and value addition. The goat farming and dairy farming courses are conducted on distance education mode through print media for self employment. Another course on Animal Welfare is also conducted and the enthusiastic animal activists and animal lovers get themselves enrolled for this course from the entire country.

Farm Radio School programmes are conducted with the assistance of Farm and Home Science wing of All India Radio Stations operating throughout Tamil Nadu. These programmes will be on the air for a 30 minutes duration on every Wednesday, for a period of 13 weeks. All the listeners are registered. On conclusion of the programme, contact classes are conducted at the university for the registered farmers.

Means of Outreach

A well equipped video laboratory available in the Department of Communication and Entrepreneurship and the video lessons prepared and distributed to the training centres, information centres, NGOs and line departments serve as the means of reaching out to the livestock farmers and end users. Books related to livestock and fisheries are published and being distributed for sale through district centres and the Agricultural Technology Information Centre.

An Agricultural Technology Information Centre is established at Kattupakkam for providing services, products, and information through single window delivery system under the financial support of National Agricultural Technology Project of ICAR. Rural Information centres located at Madurai, Trichy, and Vellore also fulfill the information needs of the farmers.

Training, mass campaign, exhibition, Farm Radio School, farm publications, Farm Advisory Service, demonstration, livestock show, extension talk, marketing linkages, input arrangements, organising farmer forums, distribution of publications and village adoption are some of the outreach activities of the Veterinary College at Namakkal.

Index